WHAT EVERY WOMAN WISHES HER FATHER HAD TOLD HER

Byron & Robin Yawn

HARVEST HOUSE PUBLISHERS
EUGENE, OREGON

Cover by Koechel Peterson & Associates, Inc., Minneapolis, Minnesota

Cover photo © Getty Images / Jupiterimages / Polka Dot / Thinkstock

All emphasis in Scripture quotations added by the authors.

WHAT EVERY WOMAN WISHES HER FATHER HAD TOLD HER
Copyright © 2013 by Byron Forrest Yawn
Published by Harvest House Publishers
Eugene, Oregon 97402
www.harvesthousepublishers.com

Library of Congress Cataloging-in-Publication Data
Yawn, Byron Forrest.
    What every woman wishes her father had told her / Byron Yawn and Robin Yawn.
        pages cm
    ISBN 978-0-7369-5043-5 (pbk.)
    ISBN 978-0-7369-5044-2 (eBook)
    1. Christian women—Religious life. I. Title.
    BV4527.Y39 2013
    248.8'43—dc23
                                                                        2013010161

Printed in the United States of America

13 14 15 16 17 18 19 20 21 / VP-CD / 10 9 8 7 6 5 4 3 2 1

To our precious daughter
Lauren Elizabeth Yawn
The sweetest human being we've ever known
and
my mother Debbie

Contents

THEN—TWO YEARS OLD

AN OPEN LETTER TO MY DAUGHTER

(And a Veiled Exhortation to Christian Fathers
and Young Adult Christian Men Everywhere)

Dear Lauren Elizabeth,

In a box somewhere in the garage there is footage of the two of us. Although it's lost in storage, it streams in my memory. I am holding you. You fit neatly in my two hands. My heart fits perfectly around your little finger—small as it was. It is a long time ago. It is the embodiment of that worn-out metaphor we reach for to describe fathers and daughters. "Tied around fingers" or something like that. Clearly, I am entwined. I've always been. Quietly, I bend down and whisper something to you. It's hard to make out what I'm saying on this fuzzy old tape. But, I know exactly what I said. I've been saying it for 14 years. You have heard me say it in word and deed every day since. "You will always be this child here in my hands. I will never leave you nor forsake you. I love you." It is 14 years ago, but it is easily today.

One day, if God wills, you will know how deeply a parent loves a child. It is a bottomless vein in a parent's heart. But you will never know how intensely a father loves a daughter. It's hard to put into words. It is a mixture of strength and softness unique to this bond. A father's love hovers like a citadel over the untouched treasure of his daughter's life. (This is why your dad acts like a suspicious sniper around you.) A daughter thrives within its safe barrier. A father's love for his daughter is a preservative against a thousand ills seeking to infect the innocence of her life.

Is it any wonder ladies are reduced to tears as they look back on the landscape of their life and cannot see a father's sweetness? It is a deep regret…and needless. Girls need dads. Neglect here is cruel. The worst thing a dad can do sometimes is nothing. It seems I counsel the ubiquitous broken young lady on a weekly basis. She is the lost young woman who seeks self-worth in the affection of a young man—never having received it from dad. Hers is a deep pain. Tenderness is a sublime power in a father's hand. It is amazing what time spent showing love at 8 does for a little girl when she is 28. It builds a confidence as few things can. It is a foundation set deep in the heart.

You do not fully realize it now, but one day in the midst of life's many hardships you'll see what I've been doing all these years. You'll see what I whispered to you many years ago. In the darkness of your pain, you'll reach down and suddenly feel a foundation beneath you. I know you love me. I know you respect me more than any other man on this earth. But I have not been turning your heart to me all these years as much as to my God. My leadership of your life is intended to provide you the slightest glimpse of His awesome power over all things, including you. I know my God will steady you.

When the time comes, you will sense a steadfastness you had not sensed before. There in that moment, His love will be my greatest gift to you. A vision of a mighty God, which I have painstakingly opened to you conversation by conversation and tenderness by tenderness, will come up and catch you. My own love, incomplete and imperfect, will now make sense in the infinite shadow of His. You will bend down quietly before your life and say, "Thank you, Daddy. God is great. He has neither left me nor forsaken me." Your earthly father will be content in being overshadowed by your heavenly one. You are not mine. You are His. I will rejoice from within the cleft of His greatness as I watch my daughter worship from knees I once put Band-Aids on.

I pray that my care for you brings into sharp focus the love of our Savior. Unconditional. Sacrificial. Patient. True. Serving. Consistent. Present. I pray my sincere affection is a contrast to the many deceptions that parade as love in this world. I pray the sight of your father in broken worship of Christ gives you the courage to raise your own heart up in praise before mankind. I pray my transparent confession of sin and weakness will incline you to retreat into Christ's righteousness at the sight of your own. I pray most earnestly that you will have not merely copied your father's faith, but sincerely found the Lord Jesus Christ as the supreme object of your own.

Dear child, do not settle. Love a man who loves Christ more than you—and you more than himself. Be attracted to tenderness, lowliness, self-restraint, consistency, and sacrifice. Seek that man who carries the imprint of our Lord's cross upon his life. Love that man who does not live in fear of your emotions, but in fear of your Lord. Don't marry a boy…no matter how old he may be. Do not fall for the first young man who comes along and shows you attention. Rather, follow that man who comes along and resembles the unconditional grace of your Lord Jesus.

I am so sorry about the condition of the average young male. I regret that they confuse lust with love. I am saddened that they are more proficient at gaming than at balancing a checkbook. I cringe that they know more of sports trivia than doctrine. I apologize that they know better how to handle a gun (which is completely respectable in one sense) than how to treat a lady. I know godliness in a man is hard to find. But find it. Otherwise, you will spend your life raising the man you thought you married. The church and this culture are filled with boys masquerading as men. Let them pass.

The man you are looking for is no boy. He is a servant. He cares for your needs above his own. If I am at all the man I claim to be, you may look at your father's love for your mother and know what it is I'm describing. You should be able to recognize it when you see it. That man who will lay down his life for yours is the type of man you can easily give yours to. The man who sacrifices himself is easy to serve sacrificially.

By God's grace, I have only intended my own love to serve as a high-water mark in your soul. None except Christ's love for you will rise above mine. This way, when that man—whom I pray for everyday—comes along and exceeds your father's love, you will willingly give him your heart. And I (secretly desiring to shoot him and bury his remains in an undisclosed location) will lovingly pass on my treasure to that man who stormed the fortress of a father's love with a weapon as meager as a servant's apron.

Your Dad
1 Corinthians 2:2

Well, she was less than an hour old and Tom was God knows where. I woke up from the ether with an utterly abandoned feeling, and asked the nurse right away if it was a boy or a girl. She told me it was a girl, so I turned my head away and wept. "All right," I said, "I'm glad it's a girl. And I hope she'll be a fool—that's the best thing a girl can be in this world is a fool, a beautiful little fool."

DAISY, *THE GREAT GATSBY*

The man gave names to all livestock and to the birds of the heavens and to every beast of the field. But for Adam there was not found a helper fit for him. So the LORD God caused a deep sleep to fall upon the man, and while he slept took one of his ribs and closed up its place with flesh. And the rib that the LORD God had taken from the man he made into a woman and brought her to the man. Then the man said, "This at last is bone of my bones and flesh of my flesh; she shall be called Woman, because she was taken out of Man." Therefore a man shall leave his father and his mother and hold fast to his wife, and they shall become one flesh. And the man and his wife were both naked and were not ashamed.

GENESIS 2:20-25

I

A Man Gladly Wrapped Around a Finger

Confessions of a Dad

Confession Number One: I Don't Have a Feminine Side

F rom the start I want to come clean on several matters. First and foremost, I am not a woman. Good. I'm glad that's out of the way. I don't think like a woman and I don't really understand how women think. As is the case for most men, a woman's mind is nearly a complete mystery to me. Which brings me to this point: I realize I am at a huge disadvantage writing a book to women. Women should be very skeptical. It would be just as legitimate for me to write a book on advanced trigonometry when I barely passed algebra. Some may question my qualifications (or any man for that matter) in addressing the various issues which women face. That's a fair question. The honest answer is no. I'm not qualified. I'm certain I would not read a book on how to be a man if it were written by a woman. Which sounds like a strange admission to make at the outset of a 200-page book. But stick with me.

I don't know what it's like to be a woman, or what it feels like to live life through her soul. So I won't even pretend. Fact is, I'm still growing in my understanding of my wife, Robin, and my daughter, Lauren. I don't have a feminine side, unless you're counting my wife. This is the very reason my wife has partnered with me on this project. She does sympathize. I am cashing checks her credibility is writing.

But my aim is not to speak into the lives of women in places I've no clue about. I'm not really going there in my portions of this book.

This book is about the frameworks of security and love a dad provides (or should) a daughter, allowing her the space of self-discovery and the freedom to grow in her femininity without fear or concern. Dad is a shelter. There are things he can say and do while he has that little girl under his care that help her take flight and stay airborne over the course of her life. It is advice a daughter needs that can only come from dear old dad. This book offers an understanding of the heart of a man, which a woman needs but can only get from the humble confession of a man. A man like dad.

Being a dad is not rocket science. It's a scary responsibility, but it's not complicated. Kids want to be loved. Daughters want to be cherished. I don't want to be a reductionist here. Certainly there is more to it. Structure is important. But fundamentally, kids want their dads to love them and spend time with them. More importantly, they want their fathers near them and involved in their lives.

I have three children. Two boys and one girl. These three human beings know one thing for certain—their dad loves them. Desperately. Not only in word, but in deed and presence. I want to be near them. I love hanging out with them. There is a lot of living going down in our house. I invite myself to their lives. I am often uninvited, but I want to be in there with them nonetheless. Besides their mom, these three are my favorite people on the planet. My best friends. They know this. This makes all the difference.

Some dads are merely present. Other dads are engaged. The former might as well be absent. The compassionless father is a contradiction that is hard to fathom. But so many are. It is a sad neglect that happens rather constantly. There's no measure of the damage that is done to a child's soul by a dad simply not caring, or not paying attention. I cannot imagine abandoning my children to this culture. Leaving them to traverse this life alone is an unthinkable cruelty.

But dads do it all the time. Even those who think they aren't are. They are around. They wield their authority. They provide. Their kids are in line. But their kids are pretty much on their own when it comes to self-discovery and life. The message is "Don't mess up" or "Don't be a nuisance." But it should be "Let's go figure out this journey called life.

Let me help you find you and what you should be doing." This is the real joy of being a dad. I have so much that my kids need. So many lessons. So much wisdom to offer. I need only to start talking. You start talking early enough, your kids will listen late. You start talking too late, and you're nothing but white noise.

This book is predicated on this fundamental principle: The love and influence of a father is an amazingly powerful force in his daughter's life. If he would but pay attention, show up, care, and start speaking into her life, he would spare her so many agonies in the future. He would infuse her with an untouchable confidence in who she is supposed to be and the courage to face life by faith. To dads I say, "She is right there. Stoop down, dad, and love that little creature. She will hang on your every word. What you tell her at twelve will save her enormous pain at twenty-two." To her I say, "I'm praying your dad takes the time to stoop."

There are so many things daughters—deep in life—wished their fathers had told them. So many lessons. There are so many daughters who wish their father had filled this space in their life. At the very moment daughters struggle against the gravity of their adolescence needing an abundance of compassion from the one man who knows them best, dads check out and leave their daughters to strive alone. Many dads have no patience for the complicated world of a teenage girl. Or they dismiss their daughter's struggles as unimportant. More emotion than substance. This is a mistake. These are the headwaters of her life, where the stability of his life is most needed. She needs her father to step in at this moment most of all and not back away. She needs him to start talking.

Years ago I started investing in a relationship with my daughter in the hopes that when the time came it would pay off. From the very moment she was born I began working toward one outcome—I wanted her to trust me in such a way that she could turn to me in the folds of life. I wanted to live and relate to her in such a way that she would view me as a compassionate and constant sanctuary for her life. I wanted her to trust me even at those moments she could not understand me, or did not agree with my counsel. I prayed that when her desires collided with the counsel of her dad in a fog of youthful rebellion she would be persuaded by the constancy of my unconditional love to lay down her arms and rest in her dad. I have tried to be the type of man she could trust with her very life and soul even when on the face of things my counsel made little sense. So I set out building a friendship. Today she is among the closest friends I have. My investment of compassion and time has paid off in huge ways. She is among my greatest treasures.

It's here that most dads blow it. They forget to like their kids, not just raise them. They forget they're raising adults and not children. They forget to start talking. When they finally do speak up and begin the conversation with their children, it's usually at the very moment they need to start walking on their own. Way too late. In a parent's panic all that comes out are lectures, prohibitions, and "No." Dads who should have been running beside their kids' lives all along, are struggling to catch up. Rather than having guided their children to the gateway of adulthood, they left them to figure it out on their own. It's a painful bit of irony when parents erupt in anger at the poor choices their teenagers make. The same human being who is frustrating them now had no alternative wisdom on which to lean.

I have refused to let my children alone. I have wedged my way into their lives from every possible angle. I have been talking nonstop—especially to my daughter. Through all of my conversations with her over the years (and they have been many), I have been laying a foundation of love and wisdom she could stand on as she came upon those transitional moments in her life. I always knew the time for significant input was limited, especially with her. There would come a time when what I had told her about life would have to suffice. A moment when she would have to make decisions on her own. Every parent knows this moment is coming with their children. When it does, we get down on our knees and pray that something sticks. We pray they listened. There are so many choices ahead of my sweet girl that she will have to make alone.

For me, one choice rises above them all. A man. The man she will devote her heart and life to. I have surrendered to the fact that I cannot choose the man my daughter will fall in love with and marry. But I have tried ever so diligently to shape her understanding of what that man should look like by exemplifying it in my own life. For this—and many other reasons—I have kept showing up in her world.

But despite all my many efforts, I knew the day was coming when she would pedal faster than I could run. I realized a gap between our genders would finally stretch beyond the innocence of her youth. There was always this inevitable threshold on the horizon moving toward our relationship where she would cease being a child and emerge as a young woman. I've known this season would require more of her mother's insight and sympathy than mine. In the same way, a mother cannot give a son all he needs. There is a point at which the counsel a dad gives his daughter cannot possibly cover the totality of her life. Indeed, I do not speak *teenage girl*. Her mother is the only multilingual person in our house. She's often my translator. There are certain conversations I cannot have with my daughter. This is not my role in her life. I respect the relationship she has with her mother. But I am still there just out of the corner of her life, watching things take shape.

More often than not I've no clue what she's "feeling" or why she is feeling it. This is true for about almost anything. I usually don't have a clue why she's crying. Or how something I said to her in passing three months back has upset her in the last ten minutes. Or why the boy who pays her no attention at school upset her because although he has no clue, she wants him to pay attention to her. I don't get any of this. Admittedly, there are so many things about this wonderful creature to which I cannot relate. She's an enigma.

But she does not need me to understand it all. She simply needs me to accept her despite my inability to understand her. A dad doesn't have to pretend to get everything that's going through his daughter's mind and heart. Because he doesn't. But he cannot pretend to care. She needs him to care whether he understands or not. So much depends on a dad being sensitive and tender even when his daughter's world is lost in translation.

You don't treat girls like you do boys. Not exactly an original observation I know, but dads too often expect girls to react like sons do.

Probably most dads would like it if they did. As it is, dads scratch their heads wondering why the tactics used on sons end up backfiring with daughters. There are different strategies for raising boys and girls. Girls don't react to dad like boys do. Their respective needs are no less intense, but they are of a different quality. The dad who does not understand this will eventually pay for it.

So often I have seen dads treat their daughters like they would some common nuisance. Intolerant of the shifting emotions that accompany her adolescence, they tend to appease her more than engage her. To him she is a complicated bundle of emotions and feelings they've neither the time nor patience to unravel. There's no way to measure the impact of this kind of neglect. It is the exact wrong thing to do with a young female heart.

Boys are like bent nails that you spend the majority of your life getting as straight as you can before they head off into the world. You apply pressure at various points in their life, give them a clear self-awareness, stay present, point them to Christ, and send them out to conquer the world. Dads are naturals with bent nails.

Not so with girls. Girls are more like precious vases placed in the hands of Neanderthals. "What do you do with this?" The wrong kind of pressure can be detrimental to a girl's growth and development. Not that females are endowed with a fragile psyche, but daughters do require a certain delicacy. The pressure you apply to their lives has to be far more precise. *Loving a daughter's heart is a skill a dad has to learn.*

Confession Number Two: There Is a Double Standard

Second, there is a double standard when it comes to raising girls. I realize I'm outing dads everywhere in admitting this, but it is true. Girls have it tougher when it comes to dad and the rules that govern her life. My own daughter has come to realize this and has pointed it out on numerous occasions. But there is a good reason for the inequity.

The world is a dangerous place, and she is an especially threatened species. My job—the bulk of it—is to protect her. (My job with her brothers is to protect girls from them until they are ready to protect girls themselves.) Honestly, this would be true whether I were a Christian father or not. This is because it's built into a dad's DNA.

There's a saying. It's crude, but it's true. When you have a son you only have to worry about one penis. When you have a daughter you have to worry about all of them. A faithful dad works tirelessly to preserve an innocence around his daughter's life and then fills his days walking the parameter of that innocence prepared to fend off interlopers. In certain ways my daughter has as much freedom and/or restrictions as her two brothers do. But I watch over her life with a much greater diligence.

A dad who fails to surround his daughter's life with his love and watch over its boundary inevitably exposes her to the cruelty of a world in which there are many who view her as nothing more than recreational equipment for sex. That's brutal, but that's the truth. Dads who can't imagine intentionally handing their daughters over to such wickedness do it indirectly. They toss their daughters into the gristmill of the culture simply by neglecting them.

So yes there is a double standard. And it has been hard on my daughter at times. But hopefully one day my daughter will thank me for the very moments in her life she most resented me. And no, I do not apologize for it. I am her champion.

Confession Number Three: All Young Men Are My Enemies

Third, in my opinion, a lot of young men are perverts. I can hear moms and dads objecting on behalf of their sons. "My son is different." Yeah, and a unicorn just ran through my backyard as I was writing this. As far as I am concerned, most adolescent boys are the embodiment of evil intent on harming my daughter by taking advantage of her. I don't like them.

Obviously there are exceptions. I'm sure there are some. But on the whole, I loathe them. They are my mortal enemy. Even the more decent ones. Even those who attend church with their mothers. I live in constant suspicion of them all. I have to. No self-respecting dad would do otherwise. They are the bane of my existence. The contempt I have for them is hard to describe. Let's just say part of my research for this book was viewing the *Taken* films with Liam Neeson. My favorite scene is the phone call. For fathers of daughters, it's our Knute Rockne speech. Neeson warns his adversary that he has skills. They're special. And that if his daughter is not let go, he will pursue, find, and kill the captor. I usually black out from excitement at this point.

I can't believe Neeson did not get an Oscar for that. It makes me cry every time I see it. I dream of picking up the phone one day as some unsuspecting suitor calls to ask my daughter out on a date and quoting it verbatim. Man! That's going to be awesome.

I feel this way about young men because I was once one of them. I was once one of these creatures I despise—a teenage boy. So I know what lurks in their hearts. It ain't always good. And this makes me very angry.

I remember talking to my daughter as she had just begun to discover boys. Just about the time they were discovering her. She was so innocent and naïve. A lamb to the slaughter. I sat her down at our kitchen table and had a rather direct conversation with her. "Lauren, you need to know that boys are perverted and only want one thing." She looked at me for a second and asked, "What? What do they want?" For the next five minutes I filled her in. It was Liam Neesonesque.

When I finished, the look on her face was one of sheer horror. Like when you tell some unsuspecting person with a mouth full of hot dog what they are really made of. In my opinion it's one of the best talks we've ever had. In her opinion it's one she wished she could erase from her memory bank. Regardless, it had to be done.

Lest I be unclear, I am not a big fan of the male species. I don't speak highly of them in this volume. And this puts me in somewhat of a tough spot since I wrote a book on men (the companion to this one) in which part of my argument was a refusal to buy into the stereotype laid upon men by the culture. The stereotype that says men are lazy slugs who think only about sex and waste their lives playing video games.

I actually have a lot of hope for men. God can do great things with them. I know many honorable men. But, honestly, there is a little bit of truth in every stereotype. There is a part of me that wants to apologize to my daughter for the condition of men in our culture. I spend much of my time with her making sure none of them get near her. Fact is, there aren't many mature godly young men out there. They are hard to find. It's difficult to say, but it's the truth.

Without the cross of Christ dominating our lives, we men are capable of fulfilling every stereotype for which we are known. Generally, men are completely unprepared to handle the heart and life of a woman. We do go into marriage and relationships thinking primarily about sex and not much else. We do have a tendency to neglect our responsibilities as we escape into recreation or video games. We do mature much later than women. It's all true on a certain level. I hate to admit it, but it is. We have not done our gender any favors.

Therefore, this book is primarily aimed at talking young ladies out of a huge mistake. It's a warning to them about guarding their hearts and thinking beyond their emotions as it concerns giving their life over to a spouse. This book is heavy on counsel about what to look for in a man and how to survive in marriage. Be warned. It's all pretty direct. Like how a father should talk to his daughter.

WHERE A DAD'S LOVE FITS

It is hard to capture the importance of a father's tenderness and love for his daughter in words. Maybe images are better than descriptions. It is a citadel. A shelter. A refuge. However you describe it, its effects are undeniable. Those young women who've had a gentleman and leader as a father are different altogether. There is a sense of security permeating their spirit. A confidence that does not rise from self, but from the years of unconditional love emanating from this man cradling her life.

The impact is no less noticeable in the men who have the privilege of having daughters. If they have served the delicacy of this creature as they should, they will be better men for it. The bond shapes a man's heart. It is a bond that never ceases. Years later, when his strength is gone and his days are few, she will visit him in his twilight. She will kneel down beside him and whisper, "Daddy. It's me." He will glow. No one else can do that.

Reciprocally, there is nothing else that fits that sweet girl's heart like his heart. A daddy's love is a key that opens a treasure of affection intended for him alone. This unconditional love pouring out of her soul slays him. To say that a dad is wrapped around a daughter's finger does not even come close to capturing the reality. It is a suitable bondage of affection. It should be.

I'll let you in on something. Fathers don't consider this a blind spot at all. Or a weakness. Of course they are wrapped around her finger. They view it as a duty and a joy. In my case, my wife rolls her eyes and calls me soft. I own this criticism. Melted is more like it. This is the one occasion in my life that the softer I am, the more force I assert.

Her two brothers are often aggravated by the preferential treatment their sister receives from me. I have shooed them off my lap innumerable times to make room for her. There is always room for her. And maybe preference. After all, my boys smell of goat half the time. Who would not prefer the company of this precious creature who seems always to smell of soap and berries? Our boys are also put off by the strict set of laws that govern their behavior with their sister. It is inviolable and tilted to her advantage. They are not allowed to lay a hand on her. She may torment them mercilessly (and often does), but they dare not lift a hand in retaliation. Dad is her ever-present guardian. She also has her own private area of the house. Especially that most prized region of her domain—that place where the rest of the family too often waits on her to emerge—the bathroom. Looking natural is hard work. And time consuming. The boys, on the other hand, share a bathroom with their parents. This arrangement has challenges of its own. Mainly for mom and dad.

Undoubtedly, her list of privileges and exemptions is longer than theirs. But my sons are not actually jealous. Over the years they have come to respect this bond between their sister and me. My love for them is not less. They get this. And I know, as a matter of fact, that their sister is no less a treasure to them. Secretly, I have intended my affection for their sister to serve as a model for my boys. I have sought to plaster a conviction about how women ought to be treated on their hearts by my ever-present delicacy toward her.

For I see them not simply as boys but as future husbands and fathers. I know what battles they face as it concerns a frame of reference for the opposite sex. Out there somewhere are young women who will place their hearts in their hands in the very near future. I intend to soften our boys' hearts and hands between now and then.

The adage is true: When a daughter cannot find love in her father, she will find it where she can. I see it lived out almost constantly in this world of ours. But it is equally true (and probably greater) that the more love she finds in her father, the more determined she will be to find that same type of love in the future.

My love is a firewall for my daughter's heart and life. One day when that man steps forward to make her his own, nothing less than sacrificial love will get through to her world. Anything other will make little sense to her. She will know instinctually whether he is a servant or despot, man or boy, leader or coward. It's not that she will love her future husband less than she loves her father. It's more that she will be drawn only to that love which bears the same qualities as her father's. As his is drawn from the gospel.

My beloved is mine, and I am his; he grazes among the lilies. Until the day breathes and the shadows flee, turn, my beloved, be like a gazelle or a young stag on cleft mountains. On my bed by night I sought him whom my soul loves; I sought him, but found him not. I will rise now and go about the city, in the streets and in the squares; I will seek him whom my soul loves. I sought him, but found him not. The watchmen found me as they went about in the city. "Have you seen him whom my soul loves?" Scarcely had I passed them when I found him whom my soul loves. I held him, and would not let him go until I had brought him into my mother's house, and into the chamber of her who conceived me. I adjure you, O daughters of Jerusalem, by the gazelles or the does of the field, that you not stir up or awaken love until it pleases.

SONG OF SOLOMON 2:16-3:5

Sarah died at Kiriath-arba (that is, Hebron)
in the land of Canaan, and Abraham went in
to mourn for Sarah and to weep for her.

GENESIS 23:2

2

LIFE—YOU'RE NOT CRAZY

T here is this young lady whom I've observed out of the corner of my experience all these years as a pastor. The best description of her I can offer is *searching*. Whatever tenderness was needed from her father went missing. So she's gone looking to fill this void her father left. Never daddy's little girl, she'll take what she can get. She would easily trade her innocence to know the slightest amount of affection and would bargain her soul for the fleeting attention of the first young man who makes the slightest effort to notice her. You see it all the time. We all know this creature. As it is, so many young tragedies started as desperate expeditions for a father's love. She thinks she's crazy. She is not.

Then there's the middle-aged daughter with a family of her own deep in the routines of life. We all know this woman as well. We were raised by a version of her. Eyes in the back of her head. Savvy. Ridiculously consistent. Stable. Steady. Somehow bringing the loose ends of every day together into a tapestry of reliability.

Her presence ensures an adult is always around, as well as a nurse, chef, chauffeur, and referee. Once a year we toss her a "Thank you" on Mother's Day, and then take her for granted all the other days. A thankless role strangely fueled by thankfulness.

This woman is awesome. A place of refuge. On the surface of her life, all is well. But fissures lay hidden beneath all that strength. Years into her own life, buried in all the duties, lies a need to be cherished by her husband. Like when they first met. A tenderness has gone missing. She lingers on it from time to time. When she does, she thinks she's being petty. She is not.

A NORMAL AFFECTION

The message both these women—at opposite stages of a similar life—need to hear is the same: You're not crazy. This need you have for affection and to be cherished by a man is normal. It is by design. And not a weakness at all. It is part of your true beauty and a feature wired into your person. By it you have the power to place a finishing touch on a man's life and complete so many other experiences.

To want to be wanted and wed is not a bad thing at all. Nor is it to be resisted. It is an innate quality of dependency endowed by the Creator from the beginning. It is woven into the fabric of who you are. It cannot be denied. You are not crazy at all. Overly emotional? Perhaps. But not crazy.

The Bible affirms the desire to be desired, romance between lovers, and a woman's need to feel safe within the protection of her man. Have you ever read the Song of Solomon?

> My beloved is mine, and I am his;
> he grazes among the lilies.
> Until the day breathes
> and the shadows flee,
> turn, my beloved, be like a gazelle
> or a young stag on cleft mountains.
> On my bed by night
> I sought him whom my soul loves;
> I sought him, but found him not.
> I will rise now and go about the city,
> in the streets and in the squares;
> I will seek him whom my soul loves.
> I sought him, but found him not.
> The watchmen found me
> as they went about in the city.
> "Have you seen him whom my soul loves?"
> Scarcely had I passed them

when I found him whom my soul loves.
I held him, and would not let him go
    until I had brought him into my mother's house,
    and into the chamber of her who conceived me.
I adjure you, O daughters of Jerusalem,
    by the gazelles or the does of the field,
that you not stir up or awaken love
    until it pleases
                        (Song of Solomon 2:16-3:5).
I came to my garden, my sister, my bride,
    I gathered my myrrh with my spice,
    I ate my honeycomb with my honey,
    I drank my wine with my milk.
Eat, friends, drink,
    and be drunk with love!
I slept, but my heart was awake.
A sound! My beloved is knocking.
"Open to me, my sister, my love,
    my dove, my perfect one,
for my head is wet with dew,
    my locks with the drops of the night."
I had put off my garment;
    how could I put it on?
I had bathed my feet;
    how could I soil them?
My beloved put his hand to the latch,
    and my heart was thrilled within me.
I arose to open to my beloved,
    and my hands dripped with myrrh,
my fingers with liquid myrrh,
    on the handles of the bolt.
I opened to my beloved,

but my beloved had turned and gone.
My soul failed me when he spoke.
I sought him, but found him not;
    I called him, but he gave no answer.
The watchmen found me
    as they went about in the city;
they beat me, they bruised me,
    they took away my veil,
        those watchmen of the walls.
I adjure you, O daughters of Jerusalem,
    if you find my beloved,
that you tell him
    I am sick with love.
What is your beloved more than another beloved,
    O most beautiful among women?
What is your beloved more than another beloved,
    that you thus adjure us?
My beloved is radiant and ruddy,
    distinguished among ten thousand.
His head is the finest gold;
    his locks are wavy,
        black as a raven.
His eyes are like doves
    beside streams of water,
bathed in milk,
    sitting beside a full pool.
His cheeks are like beds of spices,
    mounds of sweet-smelling herbs.
His lips are lilies,
    dripping liquid myrrh.
His arms are rods of gold,
    set with jewels.

His body is polished ivory,
   bedecked with sapphires.
His legs are alabaster columns,
   set on bases of gold.
His appearance is like Lebanon,
   choice as the cedars.
His mouth is most sweet,
   and he is altogether desirable.
This is my beloved and this is my friend,
   O daughters of Jerusalem
      (Song of Solomon 5:1-16).

THE UNDENIABLE BOND OF ONENESS

There have been moments over the course of my marriage where this instinct has been demonstrated by my wife. Various circumstances have created a vacancy of strength in her intended to be filled by me. There is an assortment of near misses that families experience from time to time. A serious onset of illness with a child when I was out of town. An accident on the interstate (or a flat tire) when I was across town. Sounds in the middle of the night. And then there were some tragedies that did not miss us. The loss of twins at the twenty-sixth week of pregnancy. Two broken souls.

In all these events, one instinct in her—surpassed only by her trust in God—came through. She needed me. Not just to change a tire, but to be there. Not just to offer spiritual clichés about God's sovereignty, but to exemplify a trust in a sovereign God that she herself can trust. But, to the degree that it filled a space in her, it filled one in me. Those men who most desire to be this man for their wives are closest to the intention God had for manhood. Such is a oneness of flesh. Cleaving.

When my father died some 15 years ago, so many things in my world came dislodged from their normal place. I had never really seen grief before. From a distance maybe. A glimpse here and there, but never nose to nose. Observing the pain of my mother brought me close enough to feel its breath upon my own soul. I was right up in its face. Or, maybe it was in mind. Never again have I taken death, or its effect upon a person, for granted. *Widow* is not some throwaway term for me.

The bond of husband and wife is a mysteriously powerful force. I've not seen much like it in all my years in ministry. Its power is subtle and often not felt until way into marriage. Two people become one person more and more over time as they are pressed together by experiences both good and bad. They don't even notice how deeply they've been pressed into the fabric of each other's life. Eventually they are finishing each other's sentences and thinking each other's thoughts.

When death (or divorce) finally invades, it always pulls at the fabric of that soul left behind. It's as if part of the remaining spouse was torn away. It's not a cut. It's a tear. The disorientation can be extreme as one person learns to look at life through one set of eyes and not two. This was true in the case of my mom. From that day forward her soul walked with a slight limp.

When "Doc" left this earth, my mother was overwhelmed with loneliness. There was no other person on the planet, or any number of them for that matter, who could fill the space he left. He left a big space. The vacancy was a tribute to his life and love for her. He adored her. She couldn't sleep or stand to be alone. But she was always alone, even in crowds. She tried to continue living in my childhood residence but was unable to bear the silence of his absence. Eventually she sold it and relocated to a new home near my sister.

In the intervening days, I remember being extremely concerned for her state of mind. My sister and I worried on different levels and about things no child should ever have to worry about. It was here at the precipice of my mother's pain that I learned how deep the need of a wife for her husband really is.

One day my mom walked out the front door. Without saying a word, she got in her car and headed west down the interstate. Concerned, I got in my car and followed. As I had suspected, she got off the interstate, took a few turns, and entered the cemetery where my father had been buried only a few weeks before.

I trailed behind and parked out of sight on a hill overlooking the place where my father lay. She sat in her car for the longest time. Finally she emerged, walked over to my father's grave, and lay down right on top of it. Right above him. As close to him as she could get. Looking up at the blue sky, she lay there and wept. Eventually she cried herself to sleep. A half hour passed. She got up, touched the turned earth one last time, got back in her car, and drove home. Right before she got in the car, she looked directly at me—where I had assumed I was well hidden—and waved. She knew I was there the whole time.

The scene reminded me of Abraham's grief over Sarah's death— "Sarah died at Kiriath-arba (that is, Hebron) in the land of Canaan, and Abraham went in to mourn for Sarah and to weep for her" (Genesis 23:2).

We've never spoken of this moment. I've never felt the need to ask her why she had done this. I did not have to. I knew why. It required no explanation. It was the sheer pain of grief. The love of her life undone by life itself. Her actions did not strike me as strange. They made complete sense. As I was perched above her on that hilltop, I got it. She was not crazy at all. She was a wife.

"A lady's imagination is very rapid; it jumps from admiration to love, from love to matrimony in a moment."

JANE AUSTEN, PRIDE AND PREJUDICE

Husbands, love your wives, as Christ loved the church and gave himself up for her, that he might sanctify her, having cleansed her by the washing of water with the word, so that he might present the church to himself in splendor, without spot or wrinkle or any such thing, that she might be holy and without blemish. In the same way husbands should love their wives as their own bodies. He who loves his wife loves himself. For no one ever hated his own flesh, but nourishes and cherishes it, just as Christ does the church, because we are members of his body. "Therefore a man shall leave his father and mother and hold fast to his wife, and the two shall become one flesh." This mystery is profound, and I am saying that it refers to Christ and the church. However, let each one of you love his wife as himself, and let the wife see that she respects her husband.

EPHESIANS 5:25-33

3

LOVE—FIND THIS MAN

There is no such thing as a soul mate. That is to say, there is not a specific person out there wandering around whom you must find. No man out there without whom you will never know true happiness. There is no matching version of your soul out there like some missing sock that becomes a pair only when discovered. No *yin* to your *yang*. He does not exist. Sorry to burst your bubble, but that's a myth. And a dangerous one at that. For some it has led to despair and missed opportunities staring them in the face. For others it's served as a justification as to why existent marriages should be dissolved. "I found my soul mate." That's nonsense. There is no such "happily ever after" as exists in the tidy little endings of romantic comedies. That's naïve. Consider this:

> The idea of the "soul mate" has permeated American society. American movies, songs and television shows celebrate the idea that there is that special someone for us destined by Fate who was made for us and will make us complete. The religious among us are especially vulnerable to this notion, although there is no scriptural basis for it in the Old or New Testament. But even the non-religious have been known to fall for the idea that there is someone out there who will provide the intimacy, companionship and understanding they have always yearned for.
>
> The problem with the idea of the soul mate is that the notion is so subjective, emotional and ephemeral. Infatuation can

delude a couple into thinking they have found their soul mate when they are practically strangers and propel a weak liaison by two lovers based on physical attraction, charm and approval seeking into irreversible commitment.

A study by University of Virginia Sociologist Brad Wilcox supports this view that the myth of the soul mate may indeed be harmful to America. Professor Wilcox found that over 60% of men and women in the USA believe in soul mates, but these true believers are 150% more likely to divorce than the romantic skeptic.[1]

This is not to deny a certain amount of compatibility that couples find in each other. This is not a myth. But it has more to do with wisdom than serendipity. Nor is this to deny the reality of "one flesh" between couples of which the Bible speaks. But this oneness is the result of time and trials and not chemistry.

Who *is* out there is another broken human being like you ready to be served and forgiven. A person struggling against their flesh as you are yours, making headway by grace alone. A person looking for a woman he can imperfectly love and serve as each of you bring more glory to God together than if apart. A partnership of sinners saved by grace working out this mystery called marriage. He is a flawed vessel who looks nothing like the man of your dreams, but becomes that man as your dreams change to meet with reality. You should stop looking for Mr. Right. He most always isn't. He is not the man you should find.

WHEN ALL THAT REMAINS IS LOVE

When I arrived there were but a few moments left. Every previous moment lived up to here was flowing down into these few remaining. A marriage more than 50 years in the making was coming to a quiet close with the immanent and graceful departure of a wife. I had been invited into a sacred moment to provide comfort. I was tempted to remove my sandals. There was a holiness about the scene.

Mentally and physically she had succumbed to the ravages of

Alzheimer's disease. She lay there in a bed provided by hospice. Eyes closed. Laboring to breathe. Despite the physical and mental decline this woman had suffered over years, her honor was more than intact. It had been held together by the man now sitting at her side. She was loved. Quite literally, to the end. "Til death do us part" incarnate. This was the best translation of "the two shall become one flesh" I had ever encountered. Her last breath would be equally drawn out of him. He would watch it depart. This was his duty.

He did not acknowledge me as I entered, or at any time while I was present. We never spoke. We never met. I could not bring myself to distract him. It would have been like asking a soon-to-be father to step away from the birth of his child and discuss stock tips. There is no other place for him to be. Of all the days he was designed for, this was it.

Once he waited for his bride as a nervous young man at the end of a legendary aisle. It seemed to be such a long walk. There were vows exchanged and promises made. Now, so many years later, this is the moment those promises are ultimately fulfilled. Only now she is drifting away and not toward him.

On this day the distance seems so short and the time so fleeting. But her beauty seems so much greater. She is still that young bride. Her love more precious. I prayed with his adult children, offered my condolences, and left. He looked only at his beloved and held her hand. An extraordinary vigil was taking place.

I walked out and sat in my car. It was ten minutes before I cranked it. I was in between the "duties" of my day. This humble little man and his broken-down wife halted my schedule. I wanted to take it in. It's impossible to rush past a scene like this. These kinds of moments are few. As a pastor, I'm usually attempting to erase the images humanity leaves on my daily experience. There are far too many moments I wish I could forget. Divorces. Scandals. Suburban tragedies. All that madness out there. This was none of that. This was real. I sat there absorbing its nuances in that whispery type of silence you find inside of a parked car.

To be honest, I don't know what he was like as a husband. I was a stranger to him. Whether such tenderness existed over the duration of his marriage was a mystery to me. For all I know, he could have been perched at her side full of regret. Wishing he could say some things. Wishing she could hear him say them. Sadly, many endings are like that. Full of regret. We always seem to be coming to our senses way too late.

But on the other hand, he may have been this man the entire time. Either way, at this moment, he was the man he should've always been. Tender and devoted. What kept coming to me in my moment of repose was "God, make me that man." I am so far from that, but always inching toward it by grace.

WHATEVER YOU DO, DO NOT SETTLE

Find this man. The man standing vigil over that bedside. The one whose heart and soul casts a shelter of grace over his wife's life. The one who will love you when you cannot (or will not) love him back. The broken servant whose very purpose in life is to be your lover and servant leader. Find this man. Trust me—this is the man you want. The one you need. Whatever you think you're looking for, or have imagined you need in a man, this is it. In your heart you know this to be true. However you describe this characteristic (humility, grace, sweetness, servanthood), be attracted to it most. Love the man whose unconditional love toward you adds a dignity to your life. Hold out for him. Do not settle.

There will come a time when all the youthful trappings—of such great importance at the beginnings of a marriage—will fade away. When all the idealized visions of the wedding day succumb to the reality of marriage. The fade is faster than you think. Babies. Mortgages. Schedules. Laundry. Gravity. Wrinkles. Stresses. It is inevitable. A strange déjà vu is headed your way. You will look at a scene in your life and suspect you have lived it before. You have, but from the other side. As a child you looked up at it. As a mom you are looking down at it now. You have become your mother. Saying things you said you would never say. Doing things as she did them. Being in a place you determined to never be. Or maybe thankful you are like she is. We all get here.

When you find yourself at this place, two things will occur to you.

First, you will finally know the man you married. The real man, that is. Whether servant, boy, or otherwise. There may be a thousand different qualities in him you were initially drawn to. All of them noteworthy and important in their own way. Preferences are not insignificant. Physical attraction is not to be discounted. But these are not what you lean on late in life. You will find none of them at the bedside of life's twilight. Love is all that remains when all that remains is the need for it.

By love I do not mean sentimentality or romantic notions or a word used as a synonym for like. I mean a constant sacrifice of self offered unconditionally in the unreciprocated act of service to another undeserving sinner. A gritty, constant, self-forgetful impulse to do for another instead of oneself. I mean the cross.

> If I speak in the tongues of men and of angels, but have not love, I am a noisy gong or a clanging cymbal. And if I have prophetic powers, and understand all mysteries and all knowledge, and if I have all faith, so as to remove mountains, but have not love, I am nothing. If I give away all I have, and if I deliver up my body to be burned, but have not love, I gain nothing. Love is patient and kind; love does not envy or boast; it is not arrogant or rude. It does not insist on its own way; it is not irritable or resentful; it does not rejoice at wrongdoing, but rejoices with the truth. Love bears all things, believes all things, hopes all things, endures all things. Love never ends (1 Corinthians 13:1-8).

All this that Paul describes is a constant action of self-sacrifice based on the reality of Christ's love toward the individual. Love is.

Innumerable wives—who were once the eclipsing vision of their young husband's heart—find themselves invisible decades later. Unseen. Themselves now overshadowed by jobs, hobbies, or a thousand mundane responsibilities. This invisibility causes a deep pain in a wife. To be ignored erodes the substance of a woman's soul like little else. She was designed by God to depend on her husband. When he "forgets" her, a strange sense of abandonment sets in. It is a lonely spot on the dark side of marriage. Of course, she is not without hope. God is gracious. He is powerful enough to conquer his heart.

Second, you will know this author and every other person who warned you was right. You will—at that time—see what you chose to ignore when ignoring it was convenient. Of all the things you thought you needed at that time you will realize what's really needed is exactly what's missing at this time—sacrificial love. Whatever you saw in him will be gone if it is not this thing.

You have sat in front of me countless times. A middle-aged woman with regret stuck in her throat seeking counsel about her husband and marriage. She seems always to be coming to me wondering where her husband went. But he's not gone missing. He's been there the entire time. This is him. At this moment she only wishes she could trade places with that little old lady. She wants that tender little man broken over his wife's broken body.

THAT MAN BENEATH THE CROSS

Find this man. You will find him at the cross. He is not a perfect man by any means. But he is broken over his imperfection. You will know him when you see him. He loves Christ more than he loves you, but loves you as he should because of his greater love for Christ. Look on the heart of the man. All else is inconsequential. You will get down to his heart sooner than you expect.

This man's life is composed of numerous little traits flowing out of his soul, gathering around his person forming the one mosaic of a tender and thoughtful man. A door opened. A tone of willingness and not annoyance in response to your requests. An open umbrella keeping all of you dry and half of him soaked. A thoughtfulness calling for your opinion before decisions are made. A sensitivity to your preferences that drives his leadership of your life. A passion for your touch preceded only by an equally passionate desire for your friendship. A desire for your hand in prayer at life's difficult moments. A consistency in his habits and decisions that draws out your implicit trust. A respect for his person not based on any individual trait or action but based on the whole of his life.

Oblivion at the End of Aisles

Countless times now I've stood shoulder to shoulder with soon-to-be husbands at the end of aisles. Before altars. We are together waiting on the bride to enter. Everyone is at their place. There is a pause in the music. A brief and quiet prelude soon to give way to the anthem of marital bliss. At that moment, I often catch a glimpse of the groom. As often as I do, I marvel at how much he does not know but needs to. Sometimes I know the man. Other times I don't. Often I'm left wondering whether he is ready for this servitude and covenant, or whether he is as naïve as I suspect. There is so much wisdom he needs but can only gain the hard way.

This ceremony then is the exact opposite end of life from that little old man and his fading bride. These two men seem to be separated by an infinity of degrees. One is young and ambitious, rushing past the small things as he conquers the larger. The other values the small things above all else and has slowed down enough to enjoy them. He wishes he had done so when he was younger. The younger will at times be brutish and immature in his reactions. Ultimately he will wound his bride with words slung in haste and words he forgets to say at all.

The older has been humbled by life and time. There is a gentleness in his words that garners the trust of all those near him. It seems all people, especially his wife, are drawn to the refuge of his life. The younger assumes he will live forever and will have time enough to recoup lost time near the end. He has let so many precious moments pass in order to take up more pressing matters. The older now realizes how fleeting life is. Here at this moment—at the opposite end of life— he treasures every moment that remains. The younger and older are so far apart. But the one at the bedside was once waiting at the altar himself. There is hope.

SAME MAN, SAME GRACE, DIFFERENT PATH

There was another indelible scene with a husband and his wife some years later in my ministry. Another tender husband warming his heart over the remaining embers of his wife's life. This particular wife, having been married only a few short months, was diagnosed with Stage IV pancreatic cancer. She quietly succumbed to the disease around 7:30 am on a Wednesday. Sitting by her side at that moment holding her hand was her giant of a husband, Jim. He adored his wife on foolish levels. When she died they had been married to each other almost one year—for the second time.

Their first marriage ended when Abigail became involved in an affair. Eventually she abandoned the marriage, her husband, and their one child with the hopes that her lover would reciprocate and the two would be married. Her lover, a wealthy and prominent businessman in their small town, provided her with a monthly income and put her up in an apartment. She languished in false hope as he took the necessary steps to leave his own wife and family. Of course, he never did. Five years after the affair began he broke it off and restored the relationship with his wife. Abigail found herself alone, homeless, and unemployed.

The sordid affair was a public scandal. Her ex-husband, all six-feet-six and 275 pounds of him, was shamed and humiliated in this tight-knit Southern community. He had been cut down to size by it all, not nearly as tall in spirit as he was in stature. After Abigail had left him, he quietly retreated into what was left of his life. He had his daughter. He had his shame. He was angry and broken. She was a disaster and object of collective disdain. Given all she had done, she was a hard woman not to despise.

Humiliated, she trudged forward in what remained of her life. Through a temp agency Abigail was able to find a part-time job. Sitting in the cubicle next to her was a single Christian woman by the name of Linda. As the two became acquainted, Abigail began to share details from the train wreck of her life. Linda quietly and graciously listened as Abigail began to unload her burdened conscience. What she assumed was free therapy and a shoulder to cry on was a confessional booth with a righteous ear on the other side.

Once all the facts were on the table, Linda dropped the bomb. "You need forgiveness. Christ's righteous life is sufficient enough to cover your transgression. You need only to flee to His mercy. You are not unlovable. You are no more wretched than I." In sincere repentance, Abigail collapsed in the arms of the Gospel of Grace. The transformation was immediate and set into motion a series of staggering events.

I met Abigail for the first time when she ended up in my office per Linda's request. She was "seeking some counsel" on what to do with her life. It was stunning to sit in front of her and hear the whole story. This former harlot, with all her many disgraces, was now robed in the righteousness of Christ.

There is a sort of repentance that bears the undeniable characteristics of a new heart. It has a distinct sort of mournful joy to it. As someone once opined, "This type of repentance has a way of becoming more notorious than the sins from which they are repenting." Such was Abigail's life. God's grace in her cast a shadow on who she had been before. We spent several hours on several occasions seeking God's will together. In the end, she only wanted to do whatever her Lord might ask of her. In time, He asked.

It was the type of repentance that flowed out of the life of a broken king after he was involved in a similar scandal.

> Have mercy on me, O God,
> according to your steadfast love;
> according to your abundant mercy
> blot out my transgressions.
> Wash me thoroughly from my iniquity,
> and cleanse me from my sin!
>
> For I know my transgressions,
> and my sin is ever before me.
> Against you, you only, have I sinned

and done what is evil in your sight,
so that you may be justified in your words
    and blameless in your judgment.
Behold, I was brought forth in iniquity,
    and in sin did my mother conceive me.
Behold, you delight in truth in the inward being,
    and you teach me wisdom in the secret heart.

Purge me with hyssop, and I shall be clean;
    wash me, and I shall be whiter than snow.
Let me hear joy and gladness;
    let the bones that you have broken rejoice.
Hide your face from my sins,
    and blot out all my iniquities.
Create in me a clean heart, O God,
    and renew a right spirit within me.
Cast me not away from your presence,
    and take not your Holy Spirit from me.
Restore to me the joy of your salvation,
    and uphold me with a willing spirit.

Then I will teach transgressors your ways,
    and sinners will return to you (Psalm 51:1-13).

Such was her life. She taught a multitude of onlookers about forgiveness and restoration. God's grace in her life cast a shadow on who
she had been before. We spent several hours on multiple occasions
seeking God's will together. In the end, she wanted to do only whatever her Lord may ask of her. In time, He asked.

Armed with a new comprehension of love, Abigail humbled
her heart and sought out her ex-husband. It was not an easy meeting to arrange given the shattered man Jim had become. He eventually agreed. When they finally met, she asked his forgiveness with no

strings attached. When it came to her confession, she did all the talking. It was raw.

As I recall it, she knelt down before him and kissed his feet. It made me uncomfortable in an appropriate kind of way. It was hard enough to get Jim to this place, but this almost pushed him over the edge. There was no manipulation or ulterior motive. She was not attempting to remedy her financial situation. It was sheer contrition. He sensed this. Pure sincerity of love and sorrow mixed at his feet. As I looked on, he looked at me. We both, unknowingly, had our hands over our mouths in disbelief. Somehow this was more shocking than everything she had done before.

Under my counsel, Abigail sought to be reconciled to her broken little family. She presented herself to Jim tattered and knowing that rejection was justified. Amazingly, with understandable apprehension, Jim forgave her. He demonstrated an unconditional love that is—to this day—unrivaled in my personal experience. Inexplicably, with a stunned community looking on, he bought back his precious little "Gomer" from the bondage of her stain.

The love of God looks like that. The love of God is so radical and goes to such ridiculous lengths to save such unworthy people it makes God look foolish in doing so. When God's people were at the height of unworthiness as idolatrous harlots, God sent Hosea with a message of covenant love. Hosea's love became a living parable of God's love for His people. He commanded Hosea to marry the harlot Gomer—an act that would have been unthinkably embarrassing for Hosea, a righteous man. God commanded that he love her.

After bearing him children, she left him and ended up getting sold into slavery. Hosea, in utter humiliation, had to go and buy his own wife out of slavery. He looked like a complete fool for loving Gomer so relentlessly. But note this. Don't miss it. Hosea represents God. Gomer represents sinful humanity.

> The LORD said to me, "Go again, love a woman who is loved by another man and is an adulteress, even as the LORD loves the children of Israel, though they turn to other

gods and love cakes of raisins." So I bought her for fifteen shekels of silver and a homer and a lethech of barley. And I said to her, "You must dwell as mine for many days. You shall not play the whore, or belong to another man; so will I also be to you." For the children of Israel shall dwell many days without king or prince, without sacrifice or pillar, without ephod or household gods. Afterward the children of Israel shall return and seek the LORD their God, and David their king, and they shall come in fear to the LORD and to his goodness in the latter days (Hosea 3).

God extended that same radical love to us as well. Paul put it this way.

The word of the cross is folly to those who are perishing, but to us who are being saved it is the power of God. For it is written, "I will destroy the wisdom of the wise, and the discernment of the discerning I will thwart." Where is the one who is wise? Where is the scribe? Where is the debater of this age? Has not God made foolish the wisdom of the world? For since, in the wisdom of God, the world did not know God through wisdom, it pleased God through the folly of what we preach to save those who believe. For Jews demand signs and Greeks seek wisdom, but we preach Christ crucified, a stumbling block to Jews and folly to Gentiles, but to those who are called, both Jews and Greeks, Christ the power of God and the wisdom of God (1 Corinthians 1:18-24).

A SHORTER BUT PURER MATRIMONY

I had the privilege of performing Jim and Abigail's second ceremony. I remember the day. We were ready to start, but there was no sign of Abigail. When I located her in the bride's room, it wasn't cold feet that detained her, but running mascara. She had been crying at the spectacle of God's grace that was waiting on her at the end of the aisle.

It overwhelmed her. What a day that was. Husband, wife, and daughter all stood together. A trophy risen from a complete disaster.

Not long after this very moment Abigail was diagnosed with cancer. I remember getting the call. She passed so quickly. Despite the brevity, the love that was theirs this second time around was purer and deeper than any they had known at any time before. It was a well-informed kind of love. It was well short of flawless, but filled with grace and joy.

When I visited Jim on the Friday of her funeral, I saw a twice-broken man. His love for her stood out to me most. It was courageous in its selflessness. Some would call it foolish. I would call it Christlike. When he saw me, he smiled. As if to acknowledge the only other person who had witnessed that moment of tender repentance that had ultimately melted his heart of stone. A small fraternity. The portrait of their second wedding was on top of her casket. He said to me, "You have to give God the glory for letting us be together in the end." Weeping at the sight of such grace, I walked out to my car and sat there for ten minutes before driving off.

Find this man.

> I will heal their apostasy;
>   I will love them freely,
>   for my anger has turned from them.
> I will be like the dew to Israel;
>   he shall blossom like the lily;
>   he shall take root like the trees of Lebanon;
> his shoots shall spread out;
>   his beauty shall be like the olive,
>   and his fragrance like Lebanon.
> They shall return and dwell beneath my shadow;
>   they shall flourish like the grain;
> they shall blossom like the vine;
>   their fame shall be like the wine of Lebanon
>   (Hosea 14:4-7).

LT. TODD WEAVER'S LETTER TO HIS INFANT DAUGHTER

(Killed in action September 2010)

Dear Kiley, My Sweetie:

Although you may not remember me, I want you to know how very much your Daddy loves you. I left for Afghanistan when you were 9 months old. Leaving you was the hardest thing I've ever had to do. You are so very special to me sweetie—you are truly a gift from God. The best day of my life was the day you were born. Every time I saw you smile my heart would just melt. You were my sweetie—my life was not complete until you were born.

I am so sorry I will not be able to see you grow up. But remember, your Daddy is not gone. I am in heaven now smiling down on you every day. You are so very lucky to have such a wonderful Mom to take care of you. Make sure you are good for her and help her out whenever you can. Always remember to say your prayers at night and be thankful for all your many blessings. Never forget how important and special you are to so many people. We love you so very much. When you get older and start school, do your best and try to learn as much as you can about the world you live in. Always be nice and caring to others and you will discover that the world will be nice to you. But when things aren't going your way, never forget that God knows what is best for you and everything will work out in the end.

You have such a bright and beautiful future ahead of you. Have fun. Enjoy it. And remember, your Daddy will always be proud of you and will always love you. You are and will always be my sweetie.

With very much love,
Your Daddy

We must fight fire with fire. The fire of lust's pleasures must be fought with the fire of God's pleasures. If we try to fight the fire of lust with prohibitions and threats alone—even with the terrible warnings of Jesus—we will fail. We must fight it with the massive promise of superior happiness. We must swallow up the little flicker of lust's pleasure in the conflagration of holy satisfaction.[2]

JOHN PIPER

Flee from sexual immorality. Every other sin a person commits is outside the body, but the sexually immoral person sins against his own body. Or do you not know that your body is a temple of the Holy Spirit within you, whom you have from God? You are not your own, for you were bought with a price. So glorify God in your body.

1 CORINTHIANS 6:18-20

4

PURITY—THERE IS NO SUCH THING AS CASUAL SEX

T he pressure placed on young women by the culture to be promiscuous is no less than that placed on young men. It may be different, but it is no less. From every corner of her world the expectation is there. After a certain age, her doctor begins to insist that she receive her Gardasil vaccination. To decline it is looked upon as insanity. After all, every young woman will be sexually active eventually. Abstinence is mocked as an archaic naïveté. The idea of virginity prior to marriage is thought an impossibility. The possibility of restraint is considered unthinkable. Promiscuity is inevitable. Parents must accept it. Boys will always expect it. A girl has two choices. Suffer as a wallflower, or have sex.

Culturally, we're inundated with sex. Movies, entertainment, print, fashion, advertising. You can't avoid it. Sex sells. And it sells everything. Even ads for deodorant carry sexual overtones. Masking body odor is sexy? Who knew? Music videos are more and more graphic in their portrayal of sexuality. The lyrics of popular music are borderline pornographic. Television programming is saturated with it. Unless you are watching reruns of *The Waltons* or *The Cosby Show*, chances are sex is or is at least part of the plot. Sex is everywhere.

If you are going to be sexually pure in this world and save yourself for marriage, you can expect resistance. It will take courage of conviction to remain pure. All of this is opposed to a Christ-saturated frame of reference drawn from the Bible. We're warned in various places to avoid the very immoral threads running through our culture. This is clearly seen in letters of Paul—a man who dealt rather constantly with sexual reformation in the churches to which he ministered.

> Let us walk properly as in the daytime, not in orgies and drunkenness, not in sexual immorality and sensuality, not in quarreling and jealousy. But put on the Lord Jesus Christ, and make no provision for the flesh, to gratify its desires (Romans 13:13-14).

> Do not be idolaters as some of them were; as it is written, "The people sat down to eat and drink and rose up to play." We must not indulge in sexual immorality as some of them did, and twenty-three thousand fell in a single day (1 Corinthians 10:7-8).

> Walk in love, as Christ loved us and gave himself up for us, a fragrant offering and sacrifice to God. But sexual immorality and all impurity or covetousness must not even be named among you, as is proper among saints (Ephesians 5:2-3).

> You have died, and your life is hidden with Christ in God. When Christ who is your life appears, then you also will appear with him in glory. Put to death therefore what is earthly in you: sexual immorality, impurity, passion, evil desire, and covetousness, which is idolatry (Colossians 3:3-5).

The point in all of this prohibition is not to suggest that sex itself is wrong. It is not. The point is rather that the world's way of approaching it—since the beginning of time—is wrong and should be abandoned. Our culture's view of sex lacks the original freedom for which it was designed. It takes a new set of eyes to see it as something pure and good. The biblical authors are constantly bringing into focus matters of sexuality by drawing our attention to the gospel.

You'll notice in the above verses that deviant sexual behaviors and lustful distortions are not simply prohibited; they are contrasted with something greater. There is a better way to know it. The message of the Bible isn't "Don't talk about, enjoy, or freely participate in sex." Rather, it's "Sexuality can only be understood, enjoyed, and participated in with freedom when understood in its original design." Only the cross can get us there.

In the above passage from Romans (as well as 1 Corinthians 10), sexual immorality is equated with idolatry. An idol is anything we give our hearts and lives to besides God. Idolatry was our original failure. We are idolaters at worst. Human beings are so broken we are able to take a good and decent thing and elevate it to the status of a God. Something like sex. We are a sexually idolatrous race. In the very same epistle, Paul described sexual immorality in its various forms as a consequence of idolatry.

> Claiming to be wise, they became fools, and exchanged the glory of the immortal God for images resembling mortal man and birds and animals and reptiles. Therefore God gave them up in the lusts of their hearts to impurity, to the dishonoring of their bodies among themselves, because they exchanged the truth about God for a lie and worshiped and served the creature rather than the Creator, who is blessed forever! Amen (Romans 1:22-25).

It is the gospel of grace, which Paul goes on to describe in the whole of Romans, that sets us free from our idolatry.

In the Ephesians passage, "immorality," "impurity," and "covetousness" (which all stem from the same root) are contrasted with the sacrificial love of the cross. Before Paul confronted sexual sin he encouraged a change in perspective. This results from our grasping the love of God as found in the substitutionary death of Christ. Only divine love can make sex make sense. Only the cross can rob us of the selfishness that usually contaminates our understanding of physical intimacy.

In the Colossians passage, an awareness of the doctrines of union with Christ, justification, and glorification are offered as the antidote to immorality. Only with the confidence of justification and the hope of future glorification are we actually able to "put to death...what is earthly in you: sexual immorality, impurity, passion, evil desire, and covetousness, which is idolatry" (Colossians 3:5).

THE INCESSANT DECEPTION

Incessantly—by direct and indirect messages—girls are conditioned to believe being desired sexually by men is the pinnacle of self-worth. Incessantly—by direct and indirect means—men are conditioned to look at women in strictly sexual ways. The combination is tragic. Almost always, women are demeaned in our portrayal. They are objects for sexual desire. It's not their souls, or minds, or intellect on which we focus. They are somehow less than human. If a woman is not considered attractive, she's usually not considered at all.

We are a sexually deviant culture. Have a look around for a moment. The results of our preoccupation with sex are not hard to discover. There is something evil lurking in the shadows of our relaxed depiction of sex. We've a seedy underbelly.

The porn industry—which is basically unregulated—takes in over $100 billion annually internationally. Although we try, it's hard to ignore the catastrophic effects of the industry. Women are demeaned. Men suffer lifelong addictions to porn. Wives are subjected to unrealistic sexual expectations put on them by their husbands, whose minds have been filled with countless images. Innumerable marriages are destroyed. All of this is the result of our idolatrous obsession with sexuality.

Addiction to porn is epidemic. The power of pornography is no respecter of persons:

> Sexual addiction/bondage transcends all socioeconomic, racial and ethnic groups. The idea of the sexual deviant being a filthy man that crawls out from under some rock has been dispelled in recent years as increasingly more "respectable" personalities are discovered in compromising situations.[3]

Sex trafficking is now epidemic in the United States of America. When we hear about the sex trafficking industry, we typically assume it only exists in some third world context. But every single day in the cities around our country, the sexual exploitation of young girls is taking place.

According to the National Center for Missing and Exploited Children, some 100,000 to 293,000 children are in danger of becoming sexual commodities. The US Department of Justice Child Exploitation and Obscenity Section reports that 12 is the average age of entry into pornography and prostitution in the US. According to Shared Hope, 1 out of every 5 pornographic images are of children. The statistics are overwhelming. But the fact cannot be ignored. All of this moral fracturing underneath is propagated by our playful rendering of sexuality on the surface. There are consequences.

In nearly every case and with almost every portrayal of sex in our culture there is one basic message being delivered—*sex is casual*. As long as you protect yourself against sexually transmitted diseases and it's consensual in nature and you don't end up pregnant (although abortion is always an option), it can't hurt you. According to the culture, sex is a recreational activity.

If we were to believe what we see on television, a women can casually roll out of bed after a one-night stand and go on with her life. After all, it's a natural human desire. A basic pleasure. It's nothing more than this, really. With this mind-set, we've made it possible to be completely irresponsible with regard to one of the most powerful forces in the human experience. It is this casual posture toward sex that has led to the statistics mentioned above.

A HUGE MISTAKE

There's no such thing as casual sex. That is, sex is not merely an act of physical gratification with no consequences to the human soul. This is where we've made a huge mistake in our understanding of sex. The culture has taught us to view it as merely an act of physical pleasure. But, this is not the truth. Sex is a deeply spiritual reality. According to the Bible, sex affects the soul and the person at their deepest points. Sex is the most intimate a human being is able to be with another human being. This is exactly how God has designed it.

Treating sex casually damages us in ways that are hard to repair. Such is the reason young women who are promiscuous suffer with matters of self-perception and trust. It is also the reason promiscuous young men ruin their lives filling their minds with sexual images hoping that mere gratification will fill their souls. As a pastor who has dealt with both cases pretty regularly, I can tell you—there is no such thing as casual sex.

This is the exact message Paul delivered to the Corinthians: "You cannot treat sexuality cavalierly." Their culture was not much unlike ours—it was sexually saturated, only worse, if that's possible to believe. Sex was part of the pagan religion of their past. They had carried over some of their habits into their Christian life. Paul was confronting their immorality and they were justifying their casual approach to sex by suggesting it was nothing more than an instinctual desire of the body with no spiritual implications—similar to the human body's desire for food. In the same way eating food was not a moral issue, having sex was not a moral issue. It was an ordinary human impulse that had no bearing on the soul. Therefore, they reasoned, they could engage in it with whomever and whenever they wanted. That's not far removed from how modern culture thinks.

Here's Paul's response to such logic:

> "All things are lawful for me," but not all things are helpful. "All things are lawful for me," but I will not be dominated by anything. "Food is meant for the stomach and the stomach for food"—and God will destroy both one and the other. The body is not meant for sexual immorality, but for the Lord, and the Lord for the body. And God raised the Lord and will also raise us up by his power. Do you not know that your bodies are members of Christ? Shall I then take the members of Christ and make them members of a prostitute? Never! *Or do you not know that he who is joined to a prostitute becomes one body with her? For, as it is written, "The two will become one flesh." But he who is joined to the Lord becomes one spirit with him. Flee from sexual immorality. Every other sin a person commits is outside the body, but the sexually immoral person sins against his own body.* Or do you not know that your body is a temple of the Holy Spirit

within you, whom you have from God? You are not your own, for you were bought with a price. So glorify God in your body (1 Corinthians 6:12-20, emphasis added).

In other words, sex is not casual. It's not a base instinct like hunger. While it is a natural desire given by God, it is unlike any other impulse a human being has on the natural level. There is a spiritual dimension to it that is incomparable to any other experience. It is so unique that to abuse it is to sin against oneself. To put that another way, approaching sex casually damages one's soul. It has a way of emptying out a person's being. The more casual we are with it, the emptier we become.

This is because sex was designed to create an exclusive emotional and personal connection to another human being. Sex is part of the means by which the souls of a man and woman become one. Without the personal commitments of marriage framing the sexual relationship, a person will confuse sexual gratification (or providing sexual gratification for another person) for love. The result is disarray in a person's soul. This is the very reason people who were promiscuous in their adolescence often struggle to make sense of sex within marriage.

This is the very reason for the shame Adam and Eve felt in the garden. This is why their first impulse was to cover themselves and hide their sexuality. It had been corrupted by their idolatry. Since life was now oriented around the creature and not the Creator, their sexuality was oriented around personal gratification and not the glory of God on the planet.

> Then the eyes of both were opened, and they knew that they were naked. And they sewed fig leaves together and made themselves loincloths. And they heard the sound of the LORD God walking in the garden in the cool of the day, and the man and his wife hid themselves from the presence of the LORD God among the trees of the garden. But the LORD God called to the man and said to him, "Where are you?" And he said, "I heard the sound of you in the garden, and I was afraid, because I was naked, and I hid myself" (Genesis 3:7-10).

SEX IS WORSHIP

It's hard for us to think in these terms, but sex is an act of worship before God. Honestly, to put the two terms—*sex* and *worship*—in the same sentence together may seem sacrilegious (bordering on blasphemous) to many. But, sex *is* worship. I don't mean this in any pagan sense of the word, but in an essential way.

God designed intimacy between a man and a woman to bring Him glory. If we could see it this way we'd rid ourselves of a lot of confusion and pain. We would avoid pagan idolatry on the one hand, which views the experience of sex as a mere act of gratification selfishly satisfying the individual at the expense of another, and religious asceticism on the other, which fundamentally views sex as mechanical and serving the basic purpose of procreation. In each of these instances (the immoral and puritanical), sex is robbed of the spiritual dimensions hardwired into the human experience by God. In the first instance, it is reduced to a base act. In the latter, it is a regrettable obligation. But when we follow God's design for sex, it is neither immoral nor mechanical. It is worship.

Man and woman were created and placed on earth to glorify God. This is our chief end. All of life itself is supposed to be an act of worship before God. As humanity ruled over creation serving as vice regents, they reflected God's sovereign dominion over all things and glorified Him in the process.

> God blessed them. And God said to them, "Be fruitful and multiply and fill the earth and subdue it and have dominion over the fish of the sea and over the birds of the heavens and over every living thing that moves on the earth." And God said, "Behold, I have given you every plant yielding seed that is on the face of all the earth, and every tree with seed in its fruit. You shall have them for food. And to every beast of the earth and to every bird of the heavens and to everything that creeps on the earth, everything that has the breath of life, I have given every green plant for food." And it was so. And God saw everything that he had made, and

behold, it was very good. And there was evening and there was morning, the sixth day (Genesis 1:28-31).

God created women to complete a part of a man's soul that was missing without her. The same is true for how a man fits a woman's life.

The man gave names to all livestock and to the birds of the heavens and to every beast of the field. But for Adam there was not found a helper fit for him. So the LORD God caused a deep sleep to fall upon the man, and while he slept took one of his ribs and closed up its place with flesh. And the rib that the LORD God had taken from the man he made into a woman and brought her to the man. Then the man said, "This at last is bone of my bones and flesh of my flesh; she shall be called Woman, because she was taken out of Man." Therefore a man shall leave his father and his mother and hold fast to his wife, and they shall become one flesh. And the man and his wife were both naked and were not ashamed (Genesis 2:20-25).

A man and a woman united in marriage are bonded together in a unique way. As the Bible describes it, their coming together in the act of sex results in a "oneness of flesh." Sex, therefore, is a central part of the union between man and woman and fundamental in their responsibility to glorify God. The command to be fruitful and multiply given to them "in the beginning" was intended to spread God's glory throughout the earth. As the population of mankind grew and spread around the globe, the earth would become a cosmic sanctuary dedicated to the worship of God.

THE TRAGIC EFFECTS OF OUR IDOLATRY

Tragically, mankind sinned and altered the original order of things. He chose to worship himself rather than the Creator and in so doing, pulled the walls of the sanctuary in on himself. All of life was distorted. This included mankind's understanding of sex. This is why Adam and

Eve hid themselves from each other in shame and covered their loins. They were "naked and ashamed." Sex had been removed from its original purpose—that of glorifying God. It was now a means of personal gratification. As the creature became the center of his own universe, essential parts of his nature—such as sexuality—were bent in a dangerous direction. It was no longer an innocent act that resulted in the glory of God. It was a corrupt act that resulted in the exaltation of individual desire. But regardless of our corruption, the reality regarding our sexuality still remains true to human nature. It is a deeply spiritual act that was originally intended to be a selfless act of innocence before a holy God. We've been "naked and ashamed" ever since.

Sex is a complicated reality for human beings. We're confused from the start. This is no less true for Christians. Throw in the hormones of adolescence, along with the neglect of the church, and you've got a recipe for disaster. Realistically, the church's message regarding sex is no more helpful than the world's. The church has only added to the confusion by its timidity. The church is too bashful to put forth any strong convictions on the subject despite the fact we have the answer to it. We tend to back away altogether.

Generally, most churches have no strategy for helping disciple their young women in this area, or helping mothers mentor their daughters. What do most young Christian women hear from the church about sex? Sex is evil and never to be mentioned among decent people.

Basically, the church's response is the exact opposite of the world's. But it's no less damaging. The world so overexposes the subject that it's devalued down to the level of a primordial instinct. It's about gratification, dominance, and physical pleasure. Women are viewed as recreational equipment.

On the other side, the church so avoids the subject that sex becomes taboo. Young women are conditioned to be ashamed of the very feelings God intended them to have. As a result, women enter into their high school and college years caught between the extremes of overt promiscuity and secret struggles with lust. It's utterly confusing.

I once had a newly married couple confess feelings of guilt for having had sex on Sunday. I'm serious. It was hard not to laugh out loud.

Eventually I was able to dispel their superstition. This type of nonsense pretty much sums up the church's message on sex—it's bad.

One author aptly described the takeaway from evangelicalism on the subject as "Moral people are less sexual." But sex is not evil. Not even on Sundays. After all, God created it. Furthermore, sex is not something of which we should be ashamed. Again, not even on Sundays.

MORAL PEOPLE ENJOY SEX

The desire for sex is not immoral. Believe it or not, even moral people enjoy sex. The desire is a normal part of God's design for men and women within marriage. God commanded husbands and wives to have sex when He commanded them to procreate. What's more, He designed it to be uniquely pleasurable. Which is an expression of His grace, since He did not have to do this. This may be hard to comprehend, especially for fundamentalists, but the joy of sex is part of God's blessing.

By the time "churched" young ladies reach marriage, they've been conditioned to view sex as an obligation. Sex, they are taught, is more important to the husband. Men have a greater desire for the physical stimulation found in sex. For the wife, sex becomes somewhat of a secondary inconvenience and white-knuckle duty. The operational assumption is that men are *less* emotional and *more* physical creatures. So wives grudgingly fulfill their duty.

The damage done by this perspective is vast. For one, it causes wives to grow bitter by feeling as if they're merely pieces of meat. As a result, wives withhold sex from their husbands, or coldly participate in it. The husband, in return, withdraws from any meaningful communication with his wife and retreats to the "garage" of his mind. Which ends up verifying the wife's initial suspicion. Round and round it goes. By the time the cycle's complete, the couple ends up becoming a self-fulfilling prophecy plopped down in front of a counselor charged with deconstructing the confusion during the husband's lunch break.

The biblical perspective saves us from the extremes of both the world and the church. God intended sex to be a deeply spiritual (self-less) act and not a self-indulgent one. The culture can't get this, and the church rarely gets it right. In a way that is purely Christian, the physical pleasure one receives in sex results from the simultaneous service rendered by husband and wife toward one another in the same act of intimacy. Only a Christ-centered union can know this. The apostle went on to put it this way:

> The wife does not have authority over her own body, but the husband does. Likewise the husband does not have authority over his own body, but the wife does. Do not deprive another, except perhaps by agreement for a limited time, that you may devote yourselves to prayer; but then come together again, so that Satan may not tempt you because of your lack of self-control (1 Corinthians 7:4-5).

Too many young couples enter marriage with physical attraction as the *primary* basis and motivation for marriage. Now, obviously this doesn't mean we should go looking for the ugliest person we can find when we get married, but there has to be more to the relationship than physical attraction. While sex is important and should not be prudishly marginalized, it's not the enduring power of solid marriages. To think so is naïve.

Physical beauty doesn't last. If you love your husband because of his appearance, your love is conditional. If your husband engages you in conversation only because it might lead to sex, then your love is conditional. What happens to your love when beauty wanes? What happens when the youthful thrill of sex wears off with time and age? Time takes away youthful beauty and leaves us with stark realities of life.

By itself, physical pleasure as a motivation within marriage is purely selfish. One's own physical needs is the primary goal of the marital union. This perspective does not take into account the greater biblical design for marriage.

What daughters really need to know is that fulfilling sex—as God intended it—*results* from a consistently sacrificial relationship built on the principle of unconditional love. "Good" sex does not *lead* to sound marriages. To leave the spiritual realities out of the sexual relationship will only lead to frustration, confusion, and selfishness. Wives will feel used in the absence of a husband's dedicated love and sensitivity. Husbands who are forced to beg and plead for intimacy will eventually become angry. The cross has to be central to avoid these outcomes.

Sex cannot provide the type of fulfillment we imagine anyway. Only sacrificial love can. Sex is certainly part of it, but it's not all of it. When a marriage is fueled by an awareness of God's grace toward sinners, a selflessness results that sets individuals free to enjoy sex in the way God intended.

ADONIRAM JUDSON'S LETTER TO HIS FUTURE FATHER-IN-LAW

(To Mr. Hasseltine, father of Ann Hasseltine)

I have now to ask whether you can consent to part with your daughter early next spring, to see her no more in this world; whether you can consent to her departure for a heathen land, and her subjection to the hardships and sufferings of a missionary life; whether you can consent to her exposure to the dangers of the ocean; to the fatal influence of the southern climate of India; to every kind of want and distress; to degradation, insult, persecution, and perhaps a violent death?

Can you consent to all this for the sake of him who left his heavenly home, and died for her and for you; for the sake of perishing immortal souls; for the sake of Zion and the glory of God? Can you consent to all this in hope of soon meeting your daughter in the world of glory, with a crown of righteousness brightened by the acclamations of praise which shall redound to her Savior from heathens saved, through her means, from eternal woe and despair?

I know you often wish to know certainly, whether I still approve of the first step I took, and whether, if I had the choice again to make, with my present knowledge and views of the subject, I should make the same. Well, frankly, I acknowledge that I should do the same, with this exception; that I should commence such a life with much more fear and trembling of my unfitness, and should almost hesitate whether one so vile, so poorly qualified, ought to occupy a sphere of so much usefulness.

ANN JUDSON, UPON HER DEATHBED

Have this mind among yourselves, which is yours in Christ Jesus, who, though he was in the form of God, did not count equality with God a thing to be grasped, but emptied himself, by taking the form of a servant, being born in the likeness of men. And being found in human form, he humbled himself by becoming obedient to the point of death, even death on a cross.

PHILIPPIANS 2:5-8

5

BIBLICAL WOMANHOOD—
IT'S MORE RIDICULOUS
THAN YOU THINK

R achel Held Evans's book *A Year of Biblical Womanhood* released
in October 2012. Since then (and as her research was being
published in real time on her blog), her book has stirred quite a bit of
controversy. Needless to say, the modern debate regarding the role of
women in the church is a hot-button topic. In her offering on the subject, Held Evans took an unambiguous side in the debate. In so doing
she ruffled no few feathers.

A Year of Biblical Womanhood is a spin-off of a book written by A.J.
Jacobs, *A Year of Living Biblically.* In his work, Jacobs documents a year
in his life as he attempts to live according to the various commandments within the Bible regulating the life of an Old Testament saint. It's
part satire and part journalism. Evans followed suit with *A Year of Biblical Womanhood* focusing on the Bible's commandments toward women
in particular. She submitted her life to the Mosaic codes for women for
the better part of a year and ended up doing all kinds of strange things
like sitting on a roof for a day and sleeping in a tent during her menstrual cycle. This was done in an attempt to point out the absurdity
of biblical womanhood. As the publisher's promotional text explains,

> Intrigued by the traditionalist resurgence that led many of
> her friends to abandon their careers to assume traditional
> gender roles in the home, Evans decides to try it for herself,

vowing to take all of the Bible's instructions for women as literally as possible for a year.

Evans's book hit a nerve with conservative evangelicals primarily because her central concern was proving that a conservative evangelical view of womanhood is more the result of a culturally conditioned perspective than a biblical perspective. Rarely do people immediately warm to the idea that their lifelong approach to Christian living is wrongheaded. To suggest that the conservative evangelical view of biblical womanhood is erroneous—that it is the result of biblical misunderstanding and typically ends in the painful subjugation of the female gender—is a tough pill to swallow. Many have choked instead.

In reality, Evans is playing a semantic game in order to make her point. What she terms *biblical womanhood* in her book is a strict observance of the civil and ceremonial codes within the Mosaic covenant. The idea being if you say *biblical* and apply it to womanhood, you must include those regulations applied to women living under the old covenant that was ratified by Moses at Mount Sinai, is described in Exodus, and expanded upon in Leviticus, Numbers, and Deuteronomy.

She's clearly poking at evangelicals and their literal approach to the Bible. The relationship of conservatives to their Bibles is an undercurrent in the entire book and at the center of her argument. According to her, a literal approach to the Bible, as it concerns women, will result in a tyrannical misogyny and the brutal subjugation of women.

Of course, it should be noted that "literal" interpretation is not the same as "letteristic" interpretation, where every word—whether figurative or not—is taken literally. This leaves no room for analogy or figures of speech. Literal interpretation recognizes analogies and figures of speech because they are literal aspects of language, both written and spoken. If someone says, "It's raining cats and dogs," we don't immediately start looking for falling animals. We understand by that expression that it's raining hard.

Literal interpretation also acknowledges historical context. That means we understand quite literally that the Mosaic code that functioned as a constitution for the nation of Israel does not apply to New

Testament believers. One comes to an understanding of this distinction between the Law and grace by reading the Bible literally. The Law (Ten Commandments and all) are not Christianity. The Law is the bad news—what we cannot do. Christianity is the good news—what Christ did for us. The Bible *literally* makes this clear.

> For sin will have no dominion over you, since you are not under law but under grace. What then? Are we to sin because we are not under law but under grace? By no means! (Romans 6:14-15).

> Likewise, my brothers, you also have died to the law through the body of Christ, so that you may belong to another, to him who has been raised from the dead, in order that we may bear fruit for God. For while we were living in the flesh, our sinful passions, aroused by the law, were at work in our members to bear fruit for death. But now we are released from the law, having died to that which held us captive, so that we serve not under the old written code but in the new life of the Spirit (Romans 7:4-6).

> The Scripture, foreseeing that God would justify the Gentiles by faith, preached the gospel beforehand to Abraham, saying, "In you shall all the nations be blessed." So then, those who are of faith are blessed along with Abraham, the man of faith. For all who rely on works of the law are under a curse; for it is written, "Cursed be everyone who does not abide by all things written in the Book of the Law, and do them." Now it is evident that no one is justified before God by the law, for "The righteous shall live by faith" (Galatians 3:8-11).

Ultimately, all the strange obligations Evans put herself under over the course of a year were completely unnecessary. Women are not measured by their performance of the Law, but by the righteousness of Christ, who fulfilled the obligations of the Law on our behalf. We are called not to the Law, but to Christ. Christ has completed the Law. Which is exactly what He said He had come to do.

Do not think that I have come to abolish the Law or the
Prophets; I have not come to abolish them but to fulfill
them. For truly, I say to you, until heaven and earth pass
away, not an iota, not a dot, will pass from the Law until
all is accomplished (Matthew 5:17-18).

I (Robin) think Evans knows that evangelicals who refer to biblical
womanhood are not encouraging the reinstitution of the Levitical code,
but she won't allow any room here. Those who argue for biblical womanhood are really arguing for Christian womanhood. If she wanted us
to change our terms, she should have said so. We're not suggesting that
we should be under the Levitical law, but Christ. Evans takes advantage of our specific language and pushes us into a corner of sorts. But
it's no real corner. It's more like an exit.

Fundamentally, according to Evans, a literal "biblical womanhood"
is untenable. As she puts it,

Despite what some may claim, the Bible's not the best
place to look for traditional family values as we understand
them today. The text predates our Western construct of the
nuclear family and presents us with a familial culture closer
to that of a third-world country (or a TLC reality show)
than that of Ward and June Cleaver. In ancient Israel,
"biblical womanhood" looked different from woman to
woman, depending on her status.[4]

Evans makes a valid point here. It is true that evangelicals have
been known to read a lot of our Americanism into our Christianity. It
should be the other way around. It's difficult for church people to separate fact from tradition. But Evans's argument goes further than this.
The implicit suggestion is that biblical womanhood is impossible. No
one does it. Not even those who say they do. That is, if you are going
to be literal and go back into the Old Testament and apply all the laws
and customs. (Clearly, Evans seems to be confused about the distinctions between the Mosaic covenant and the new covenant. But we'll
grant her the point for the sake of argument.)

According to Evans, biblical womanhood, at its most literal, ends up being an absurd sort of burden. The irony here is obvious. Evangelicals, who take being biblical so seriously, would never submit themselves to a literal view of biblical womanhood. Clearly, Evans's aim is to dismantle the traditional notion of biblical womanhood by exposing the hopelessness of an actual application. In her own words,

> Now, we evangelicals have a nasty habit of throwing the word biblical around like it's Martin Luther's middle name. We especially like to stick it in front of other loaded words, like economics, sexuality, politics, and marriage to create the impression that God has definitive opinions about such things, opinions that just so happen to correspond with our own. Despite insistent claims that we don't "pick and choose" what parts of the Bible we take seriously, using the word biblical prescriptively like this almost always involves selectivity.

> After all, technically speaking, it is biblical for a woman to be sold by her father (Exodus 21:7), biblical for her to be forced to marry her rapist (Deuteronomy 22:28-29), biblical for her to remain silent in church (1 Corinthians 14:34-35), biblical for her to cover her head (1 Corinthians 11:6), and biblical for her to be one of multiple wives (Exodus 21:10).[5]

FROM ASSUMPTION TO FORGONE CONCLUSION

Somewhere, Evans blogged about a debate she was having with her publisher. It was over the use of the term *vagina*. This does happens from time to time. Not a debate about the word *vagina*, but author and publisher wrangling over words and phrases. It's part of the give and take of being published. Ultimately, the publisher did not allow the term to be used. Despite her protest for the sake of principle, Evans caved. All authors do. Published ones, that is. My husband and I are no exception. We've given in here and there.

But nonetheless, Evans let her angst be known via the blogosphere. In her opinion, the restriction was prudish and shortsighted. To her, this decision represented a major inconsistency in the Christian publishing world. In order to maintain a "Christian standard" in publishing, the use of a legitimate anatomical term would be avoided for fear of offense. And yet, the same publishing company will turn around and publish some bizarre argument that bears no semblance to Christianity, no problem.

I agree with her. This inconsistency is troubling. But ironically, Evans's book is a perfect example of her concern. The book is built upon a rather obvious and angry sweeping generalization that distracts from any actual discussion on the subject. Feminist vitriol is balled up in a sardonic fist and levied against traditional evangelicals.

In fact, the entire book is dependent upon a colossal false dilemma: If you believe in biblical womanhood, you are demeaning to women and out of step with the times. The concept of biblical womanhood within the book is held captive by Evans's own extreme stereotypes. The entire project is aimed at mocking traditional views of womanhood within evangelicalism. It's not that *some* views of biblical womanhood are wrong. It's that *any* view of biblical womanhood is wrong. She makes this clear.

> Those who seek to glorify biblical womanhood have forgotten the dark stories. They have forgotten that the concubine of Bethlehem, the raped princess of David's house, the daughter of Jephthah, and the countless unnamed women who lived and died between the lines of Scripture exploited, neglected, ravaged, and crushed at the hand of patriarchy are as much a part of our shared narrative as Deborah, Esther, Rebekah, and Ruth. We may not have a ceremony through which to grieve them, but it is our responsibility as women of faith to guard the dark stories for our own daughters, and when they are old enough, to hold their faces between our hands and make them promise to remember.[6]

Evans's logic flows thusly. Biblical womanhood is an unthinking and fundamentalist ecclesiastical tyranny that demeans women. No thinking woman would ever submit to it. Her tone comes off as classic elitism. Honestly, the arrogance of Americans to speak on behalf of entire cultures, reject past generations, and disqualify centuries of practice based solely on contemporary opinions never ceases to amaze me.

The author travels from assumption to forgone conclusion with lightning speed. She constructs a straw man, labels it as traditional biblical womanhood, and then sets fire to it incessantly. The only conclusion possible is hers. Sounds very much like the logic of her fundamentalist past she's so intent on rejecting.

Evans is a skilled communicator. I give her props for that. Funny and ironic? Yes. Good reasoning? No. In the end, the book only appeals to those who already share her opinion. It's ad hominem. There's no way she actually and fairly represents the other perspective. According to her, there isn't another perspective. The book is red meat for egalitarians.

And it's so unnecessary. There are so much better arguments others have offered defending her position. Right now within conservative and Reformed circles a discussion of the role of women is underway. As younger generations of women within the church are compelled to serve Christ and the gospel they are forced to deal with the Bible's meaning on the subject. What's different is that the same young women who are attempting to expand their impact and roles have an intense passion for the gospel and commitment to the authority of the local church. It would seem they have realized that their desire for gospel ministry and the structures that God has put in place are not in conflict.

The analogous effect of Evans's argument in my mind, would be the gratuitous bathroom humor that shows up in movies not having substance enough to capture the audience's attention. My husband always giggles. He tries not to, but he can't help it. I roll my eyes. Point is, there's really no need for all the over-the-top stereotyping. In the end, Evans is a feminist—which is her right—torching her tradition in order to retain the respect of her feminist peers.

SETTING FIRE TO A STRAW (WO)MAN

Honestly, this straw man Evans torches throughout her book is unrecognizable to me. It has not been my experience as a Christian woman. What's more, I choose to submit to my husband's authority and leadership because I love Christ, not because I fear I'm going to be dragged out to the edge of town and stoned to death. And, contrary to the implied connection between Evans's uniquely supportive husband and the rejection of traditional models, my husband is very supportive of my gifts and eager for my contribution.

For example, I'm a registered nurse. I still practice as a nurse, albeit on a flexible and limited schedule. I have chosen to dedicate the majority of my attention to my husband, children, home, and my husband's ministry. But it was my husband—who is a pastor, by the way—who encouraged me to stay current in my nursing. According to him, since I had worked hard for the degree and enjoyed practicing, I should find time to do it.

My ambitions here are not at odds with God's standard for our marriage. As my heart sincerely rejoices in the latter, the latter is prioritized accordingly. But mine is not an exceptional situation. This spirit is true for many families we worship with. There is no great contradiction between the contribution of a woman to a marriage or church and the structure God has ordained for both.

Sure there are crazies in every camp, but they don't define the whole camp. If we are going to think along these lines (the participants of a system of thought must be universally consistent), then we won't be a part of any group, including Americans or feminists. Abusive husbands (emotionally or physically) in no way represent the biblical standard. They contradict it. Ironically, a majority of the Levitical code was written to create social justic and protect one citizen from the other. There are also laws that require judgment against those who would take advantage of their neighbors.

Abusive and despotic husbands should be confronted and/or arrested where necessary. My husband and the elders of our church have intervened in a number of abusive husband cases over the years. This has everything to do with common sense, not to mention Christianity.

Point is, my experience has been quite the opposite of Evans's. She seems to be angry at her conservative roots. This is also evidenced by her other writings. Evidently the fundamentalist gristmill she suffered as a child did a number on her. But who doesn't have "fundie" wounds?

I refuse to allow Evans and those who argue similarly to pigeonhole me in their maligned view of biblical womanhood. She's not even close in her assessment. The examples of abuse she offers from real-life cases may have really happened, but they certainly don't represent what is really Christian.

THE BIBLICAL SYMMETRY OF SUBMISSION AND POWER

Several thoughts come to mind. First, I can't avoid the sense that Evans's protest ends up mocking God Himself. It only indirectly gets at her odd and angry caricature of biblical womanhood. After all, it's not merely the "biblical model" being shamed, but the source of it as well. And that source is God. Regardless of our views toward the laws God handed down to His people for their good in the Mosaic covenant, they are still the laws of the one true God.

Beyond the fact that Evans's views reveal an enormous misunderstanding concerning the continuity and discontinuity between the testaments, it's her brazen rejection of God that is so stunning. Okay, so she thinks biblical womanhood is stupid and archaic. And she set out to mock it and its adherents publicly and very intentionally over a year's time. Then she published her opinion and marketed it all over the Internet, national television, and through speaking engagements. She became an advocate for egalitarianism and women's rights in the church. She accomplished what she set out to do. But did it ever occur to her how disrespectful toward the God of the Bible all this appears? The blatant lack of reverence is palpable.

The Old Testament saint had a much different view of the Law of God that regulated their daily lives. Regardless of how extreme many

of the regulations may seem to us, they viewed the code of Law as free-
ing and not oppressive. They delighted in it no matter the requirement
because it was written for their good by a covenant-keeping God.

> Oh how I love your law!
>> It is my meditation all the day.
> Your commandment makes me wiser than my enemies,
>> for it is ever with me.
> I have more understanding than all my teachers,
>> for your testimonies are my meditation.
> I understand more than the aged,
>> for I keep your precepts.
> I hold back my feet from every evil way,
>> in order to keep your word.
> I do not turn aside from your rules,
>> for you have taught me.
> *How sweet are your words to my taste,*
>> *sweeter than honey to my mouth!*
> Through your precepts I get understanding;
>> therefore I hate every false way.
>
> Your word is a lamp to my feet
>> and a light to my path.
> I have sworn an oath and confirmed it,
>> to keep your righteous rules.
> I am severely afflicted;
>> give me life, O LORD, according to your word!
> *Accept my freewill offerings of praise, O LORD,*
>> *and teach me your rules.*
> I hold my life in my hand continually,
>> but I do not forget your law.
> The wicked have laid a snare for me,
>> but I do not stray from your precepts.

Your testimonies are my heritage forever,
   for they are the joy of my heart.
I incline my heart to perform your statutes
   forever, to the end (Psalm 119:97-112).

When David employed concepts like love, sweetness, free will offering of praise, and joy to describe the Word of God, he was speaking of the Law with a capital *L*. In other words, he was including the stipulations of cleanliness laid out in Leviticus. His understanding of the Law naturally included all the "bizarre" observances in the Levitical code—such as what a woman should do during her menstrual cycle. The Law was not an oppressive bondage for either men (who were equally subject to the guidelines of the ceremonial law) or women. It was a joy. The Law was good. "So the law is holy, and the commandment is holy and righteous and good" (Romans 7:12).

Furthermore, how demeaning is this entire demonstration toward the Christian woman who might sincerely and with joy submit to her husband according to that structure in marriage ordained by God? (Or, toward that ancient Old Testament woman from a Middle Eastern context who also obeyed all the stipulations of the Mosaic Law from faith and with joy, for that matter?) What about this woman? Does she not have the right to choose here? Is she just too stupid to know any better? Too simpleminded to get it? Is there really an insurmountable divide between being a submissive wife and freedom?

Again, the conclusion we are left with in all this is unavoidable. Any woman who submits to her husband is merely ignorant of better realities and in need of liberation. Her husband is more a prison guard than a partner. Am I left to assume by all this that any woman in her right mind, or who was better informed about her personal rights, would reject this archaic patriarchal system suppressing her freedom? Does the sincere conviction and choice of the individual in all of this—whether one thinks it foolish or not—mean nothing?

In the end, it appears that Evans is guilty of the very same bias she is arguing against. It's classic feminist elitism. Think in progressive ways, or be considered idiotic.

LITTLE BROKEN ENCYCLOPEDIAS OF GODLINESS

We've several sweet elderly women in our church. They're examples to the young moms and wives. Heroes to us all. We sit at the feet of their lives. Living encyclopedias of what it means to be a godly woman walking among younger generations. One in particular comes to mind. A widow. She served on the mission field of Japan with her husband for more than 50 years.

Japan, as it turns out, has a heavily patriarchal culture. For 50 years she followed, served, and submitted to her husband as they labored for the gospel in a foreign land. She went with him halfway around the world because she yielded to his leadership and trusted his sense of God's calling on their lives.

But she is not weak. She is strong and spirited. Life on the mission field forged her into one of the strongest women we have ever met. She is smart and witty. Opinionated on certain matters. No less a contributor than her late husband to their ministry. She is no pushover. A robust personality. His equal on so many levels and superior in other respects. But this woman was also unashamedly submissive as a wife.

She is a picture of the spirit of biblical womanhood—the real version, that is. Her submissive life does not make me ashamed of God's design, but it makes me want to take shelter in it. In all of her amazing strength of character, she is still a gentle creature who brought honor to her husband's life as she sought to honor God's will for her own.

Even after her husband's death she has been a symbol of honor above his life. She is proof positive to me that the two—submission and power—are not in conflict as we so often suppose. But the superior example of such symmetry is Christ Himself. All of this brings me to one question for the dissenters in this conversation: Would you have her be ashamed that her greatest ambition in life was to serve the ambition of her husband? To intentionally and willingly stand in her husband's shadow? To be thought less of? To be his helpmate until the end? I cannot help but feel the contempt progressivism has for this angelic creature.

A LOT OF WORK FOR NOTHING

But the greatest oversight here (and the saddest quite frankly) concerns the core of Christianity itself—the gospel. It's a glaring vacancy in the book. It's the same empty space found in most debates about gender roles and Christians. There's a good reason the gospel is usually conspicuous by its absence. (Unless your gospel is less evangelical in nature and more social.) You can't simultaneously describe the condescension of God in the gospel and argue for your own rights. As a result, there's no real connection in any of this discussion of the true gospel of God's grace and womanhood. For certain, the gospel is mentioned. But it's left to hang there meaningless. It's merely cliché. There's no explanation. Christianity and the gospel are assumed by the author. This makes it impossible to have any fair assessment of biblical womanhood. After all, the cross is the standard of all our conduct. This is true both for husbands and wives. Despite the consistent reference to Christianity in the book, there is a glaring disconnect between biblical Christianity and womanhood.

Does Evans recognize this? Or has she chosen to ignore it? Or is she unknowingly guilty of the very charge she makes against complementarians? Could it be that she's reading her own progressive perspective into the message of the Bible? This last question offers the only explanation for why equality and personal rights can factor so strongly in her perspective. It's hard to get there when the cross is your spectrum. Speaking as a Christian wife, is there anything more contradictory than for us to stand and demand our personal rights and power as Jesus hangs there and gives His up for us?

If Evans intended to make a biblical view of womanhood appear foolish, then she went to great lengths for nothing. It already appears foolish. The apostle Paul tells us in 1 Corinthians 1 that "the word of the cross is folly to those who are perishing" (verse 18). Even a "balanced" or "progressive" perspective of biblical womanhood will be vilified by our secular society. After all, it's a reflection of the gospel itself. The cross and its call on our lives is crazy nonsense to the world.

> Do not think that I have come to bring peace to the earth. I
> have not come to bring peace, but a sword. For I have come
> to set a man against his father, and a daughter against her
> mother, and a daughter-in-law against her mother-in-law.
> And a person's enemies will be those of his own household.
> Whoever loves father or mother more than me is not wor-
> thy of me, and whoever loves son or daughter more than
> me is not worthy of me. And whoever does not take his
> cross and follow me is not worthy of me. Whoever finds
> his life will lose it, and whoever loses his life for my sake
> will find it (Matthew 10:34-39).

If submission is involved, the culture will chew it up and spit it out
as nonsense. So let's be honest. It's not womanhood we're really struggling with here—it's the heart of Christianity and its impact upon
womanhood.

At one point Evans concludes,

> As a Christian, my highest calling is to follow Christ. And
> following Christ is something a woman can do whether
> she is married or single, rich or poor, sick or healthy, child-
> less or Michelle Duggar, mom of nineteen.[7]

I couldn't agree more with this sentiment. But based on the message of her book, I wonder whether she agrees with it. Or I'm not sure
if she sees the tension between that statement and what she says else-
where. Clearly, we have in mind two different realities as to what it
means to "follow Christ."

It's odd to see her arguing for a Christocentric perspective toward
womanhood in a book designed to debunk submission. It's strange
because Christianity holds condescension as a key attribute of both
its founder and followers. As someone wrote, "Christianity is the only
major religion to have as its central event the humiliation of its God."[8]
Normally I would applaud Evans's point above, but the contradiction
is too overwhelming. You see this, right? If Christ followed Evans's perspective—that no one should be subordinate to any other person and
personal equality is the greatest good—than there would be no Christianity at all.

In Isaiah 53 we read this:

> He grew up before him like a young plant, and like a root out of dry ground; he had no form or majesty that we should look at him, and no beauty that we should desire him. He was despised and rejected by men; a man of sorrows, and acquainted with grief; and as one from whom men hide their faces he was despised, and we esteemed him not. Surely he has borne our griefs and carried our sorrows; yet we esteemed him stricken, smitten by God, and afflicted. But he was wounded for our transgressions; he was crushed for our iniquities; upon him was the chastisement that brought us peace, and with his wounds we are healed (verses 2-5).

Christianity was founded on and through the very realities being debunked by Evans's argument. If you actually follow Christ, He leads you toward condescension and the subordination of your entire being. Every Christian ends up being the servant of every other person.

> Do not get drunk with wine, for that is debauchery, but be filled with the Spirit, addressing one another in psalms and hymns and spiritual songs, singing and making melody to the Lord with your heart, giving thanks always and for everything to God the Father in the name of our Lord Jesus Christ, submitting to one another out of reverence for Christ (Ephesians 5:18-21).

It's an incomparable inconsistency to use Christ to argue for the defense of personal rights or to demand personal equality when Christ's refusal of His personal rights (infinitely greater than ours) and equality (even though He was equal with God) resulted in the salvation of unworthy sinners—men and women alike.

All of us—wives, husbands, men, women, children, parents—who claim to be Christian are committed to His condescension as a way of life. Submission is at the heart of the gospel. It was our desire for autonomy, demand of individual rights, and unwillingness to submit ourselves to God's design that got us into this mess in the first place.

If sleeping in a tent during the menstrual cycle is intended by Evans to highlight the ludicrous nature of God's demands toward women, then those demands set on Christ by the same God are more ludicrous by infinite measures. What Jesus subjected Himself to in order to obey His Father makes a tent in the front yard during menstruation seem rational by comparison. After all, He "tabernacled" among us.

He left heaven and perfection to subordinate Himself to the wickedness of fallen humanity ultimately and willingly surrendering His life to be sacrificed for that same fallen humanity. How stupid and out of step with the times is that? He should have refused. He should have demanded His rights as an equal member of the triune Godhead. It's embarrassing, really. Or as Paul put it, "a stumbling block to Jews and folly to Gentiles" (1 Corinthians 1:23).

But it's this foolish love of my Savior that motivates me to follow and submit my life to Him. To be Christian is to subordinate your life to His because He subordinated His life in the place of yours. It's because of Christ's self-sacrificing love for me on Calvary that I obey Him and submit my life to the leadership of my husband. Biblical womanhood (and manhood) is tied to the self-denying realities of the cross.

So when we say our highest calling as Christian women is to follow Christ, let's make sure we know what we're actually saying. That's not some throwaway spiritualized expression. It's very real. If I follow Christ truly, it leads to a willing spirit of self-sacrifice and self-denial. This is where it leads because this is where Christ is. It leads to a "cross." If my Lord asked me to run through a wall, I would. Mock me, as you will. I care not. If my Lord asked me to submit my life to an imperfect leader in my husband, I will. Christ is my Lord. It is He whom I follow.

A Womanhood That Arises from Love for Christ

Ultimately, as is true with all "Christian feminists," Evans is arguing for social justice and not biblical Christianity. The womanhood of which I am versed and committed, which arises from the gospel and love for Christ, is not short on common sense, grace, or crosses.

Christ's call to obedience is counterintuitive. Up is down. Strength is weakness. Greatest is least. Least is greatest. We always seem to miss this despite the unending theme emanating from Calvary. Submission to another is not representative of an absence of power or worth. Submission is true power.

Order within Christian marriage does not mean women are lesser in nature. This is not God's economy. None has subordinated themselves more than Christ. He became lesser than all others. Was He weak as a result? Is He "lesser" in nature than His Father for this position of lowliness He occupied on our behalf? Or, from the other angle, does a position of authority mean someone is of a greater quality, or more important? Jesus prohibited such attitudes in His disciples by pointing to the example of His own life. According to Him, it only means that those in positions of authority are the first servants.

If Evans's construct of biblical womanhood is as absurd as she argues, then how much more impossible is *Christian* womanhood? Fact is, it's more ridiculous than anything Evans did in her year-long experiment. Following Christ as a woman and wife requires a sincerity of heart that is not impossible for me. With Christ it's not just the doing that is important, but the desiring. Countless people go through the motions of obedience out of a sense of obligation rather than a sense of worship. When Jesus came calling us to follow Him, He made it clear that the letter of the Law was not sufficient. It was the intent of the heart and Spirit of the Law that matters most. This, of course, is where we need the gospel of grace most because we struggle most at the point of sincerity. Merely checking the boxes on the requirements was never what God intended for His people.

Evans had it wrong from the beginning. What Christ has called women to is much more difficult than anything she attempted. In fact, doing what she did is easy compared to conforming your heart to God's desire for your life. It's much harder to be selfless and unconditional in your love for your husband than it is to sew your own clothes.

You can't do it in your own power, and only the cross of your Savior makes it make sense to you.

On February 5, 1812, Ann Hasseltine married Adoniram Judson. Two weeks later they sailed from America to India as missionaries. Ann Judson was the first American female missionary. After being refused entry into India, the Judsons established their ministry in neighboring Burma in 1813. Together, in a foreign and unreached land, they set out to accomplish their ministry goals of gospel proclamation, Bible translation, and the establishment of a church. By the time Adoniram had died in 1850, they had translated the Bible, established more than 100 churches, and were directly responsible for some 8000 converts.

In 1823, war broke out between Britain and Burma. The American missionary Adoniram was viewed as a British sympathizer and thrown into prison. For 18 months with their 3-month-old daughter in tow, Ann stayed at her husband's side in the prison some 20 miles from their home and nursed him back from the brink of death due to maltreatment. In the process of caring for him and helping to gain his freedom, Ann developed a fever. She died in October 1826 in their home. Before she died, she penned these words.

> I know you often wish to know certainly, whether I still approve of the first step I took, and whether, if I had the choice again to make, with my present knowledge and views of the subject, I should make the same. Well, frankly, I acknowledge that I should do the same, with this exception; that I should commence such a life with much more fear and trembling of my unfitness, and should almost hesitate whether one so vile, so poorly qualified, ought to occupy a sphere of so much usefulness.

THEN—WADE (4), BLAKE (3 MOS), AND "LUCHI" (6)

ADONIRAM JUDSON'S LETTER REGARDING MARRIAGE TO ANN HASSELTINE

January 1, 1811. Tuesday morning

It is with the utmost sincerity, and with my whole heart, that I wish you, my love, a happy new year. May it be a year in which your walk will be close with God; your frame calm and serene; and the road that leads you to the Lamb marked with purer light. May it be a year in which you will have more largely the spirit of Christ, be raised above sublunary things, and be willing to be disposed of in this world just as God shall please. As every moment of the year will bring you nearer the end of your pilgrimage, may it bring you nearer to God, and find you more prepared to hail the messenger of death as a deliverer and a friend.

And now, since I have begun to wish, I will go on. May this be the year in which you will change your name; in which you will take a final leave of your relatives and native land; in which you will cross the wide ocean, and dwell on the other side of the world, among a heathen people. What a great change will this year probably effect in our lives! How very different will be our situation and employment! If our lives are preserved and our attempt prospered, we shall next new year's day be in India, and perhaps wish each other a happy new year in the uncouth dialect of Hindostan or Burmah.

We shall no more see our kind friends around us, or enjoy the conveniences of civilized life, or go to the house of God with those that keep holy day; but swarthy countenances will everywhere meet our eye, the jargon of an unknown tongue will assail our ears, and we shall witness the assembling of the heathen to celebrate the worship of idol gods. We shall be weary of the world, and wish for wings like a dove, that we may fly away and be at rest.

We shall probably experience seasons when we shall be "exceeding sorrowful, even unto death." We shall see many dreary, disconsolate hours, and feel a sinking of spirits, anguish of mind, of which now we can form little conception. O, we shall wish to lie down and die. And that time may soon come. One of us may be unable to sustain the heat of the climate and the change of habits; and the other may say, with literal truth, over the grave—

By foreign hands thy dying eyes were closed;
By foreign hands thy decent limbs composed;
By foreign hands thy humble grave adorned;

but whether we shall be honored and mourned by strangers, God only knows. At least, either of us will be certain of one mourner. In view of such scenes shall we not pray with earnestness "O for an overcoming faith," etc.?

He who has great power should use it lightly.

SENECA

Husbands, love your wives, as Christ loved the church and gave himself up for her, that he might sanctify her, having cleansed her by the washing of water with the word, so that he might present the church to himself in splendor, without spot or wrinkle or any such thing, that she might be holy and without blemish. In the same way husbands should love their wives as their own bodies. He who loves his wife loves himself. For no one ever hated his own flesh, but nourishes and cherishes it, just as Christ does the church, because we are members of his body. "Therefore a man shall leave his father and mother and hold fast to his wife, and the two shall become one flesh." This mystery is profound, and I am saying that it refers to Christ and the church. However, let each one of you love his wife as himself, and let the wife see that she respects her husband.

EPHESIANS 5:25-33

6

A SPIRITUAL LEADER—
BE CAREFUL WHAT YOU ASK FOR

I want my husband to lead and I tell him to do it all the time."
I can't count the number of times I've heard some version of
this plea offered by suburban wives over my 20 years as pastor. Two
thoughts immediately come to mind. One is the irony. "I tell my husband to lead"? That's funny on so many levels and sad on others. I usually laugh out loud when I hear it. Usually I'm the only one who gets
the humor.

Often, by the time a wife gets around to expressing a frustration
with her husband's negligence, the roles within the marriage have long
been reversed. Insisting that her husband take up his leadership responsibility starts to look logical and is too often the only recourse left. It's
a strange place for a wife to find herself. A place most wives can't stand
to be or know how to get out of.

The other is the contrast. I find the above to be a rather constant
frustration among Christian wives. It's at direct odds with the progressive ideals currently being put forth in certain quadrants of the church.
If we were to believe the message emanating from modern and more
liberal branches of evangelicalism, we would have to conclude that a
demand for gender equality represents the greatest concern among
women in the church. But when I compare the extent of this concern
with my experience on the ground of ministry, it pales in comparison
to the number of humble wives who want to be led.

In other words, the exact opposite seems to represent the mind-set of most Christian women. They are not rejecting male leadership; they are desperate for it. They are weary of carrying the load of leadership intended for their husbands. Leaderless wives are an unfortunate majority in the church. In my experience, Spirit-filled and regenerate wives informed by the gospel long for their husbands to rise up as the spiritual leaders in their homes. They are ready and willing to hand over leadership. They're not jealous for it.

PAUL WAS NOT A MISOGYNIST

As the Bible would explain, this order is not the result of a long-standing tradition imposed upon modern women, but God's design for the universe. Men did not come up with it. God did. As a result, a want for leadership comes from a place deep in a woman's soul. The role of the husband as leader is not the medieval remains of patriarchy that must be rejected in lieu of modern realities. It's part of the order a caring God inserted into the universe. Paul made this very point. It goes back to the glory of creation and not the dark ages.

> I desire then that in every place the men should pray, lifting holy hands without anger or quarreling; likewise also that women should adorn themselves in respectable apparel, with modesty and self-control, not with braided hair and gold or pearls or costly attire, but with what is proper for women who profess godliness—with good works. Let a woman learn quietly with all submissiveness. I do not permit a woman to teach or to exercise authority over a man; rather, she is to remain quiet. For Adam was formed first, then Eve; and Adam was not deceived, but the woman was deceived and became a transgressor. Yet she will be saved through childbearing—if they continue in faith and love and holiness, with self-control (1 Timothy 2:8-15).

Paul was not a misogynist. In his day, arguing for the gospel of grace as he did, he would have been considered a progressive.

> There is neither Jew nor Greek, there is neither slave nor free, there is no male and female, for you are all one in Christ Jesus. And if you are Christ's, then you are Abraham's offspring, heirs according to promise (Galatians 3:28-29).

To suggest that a distinction among races, genders, and classes of people was of no benefit as it concerned salvation was a radical statement in Paul's day. It was a blatant argument for equality. But this equality did not eliminate the structure God ordained. It informed it. Both husbands and wives were to be constrained by the realities of the gospel of grace.

When Paul wrote of divine order within marriage, he was not calling for the oppression of women but their liberation. He was describing a liberty that comes from having Christ at the center of a marriage. One author describes the issue this way:

> Surely the apostle was aware of the provocative nature of his counsel. This is the same man who on other occasions campaigned on behalf of women's rights, even coining the revolutionary slogan "There is no male and female, you are all one in Christ" (Galatians 3:28). How do we reconcile Paul's advocacy on behalf of women to his jarring command to wives?
>
> There is a simple solution. It is possible that the injunction "wives submit to your husbands" was not intended to be demeaning at all. It may have even been intended to exalt the position of wives.[9]

The symmetry God intends between husband and wife is a beautiful reality. It brings Him glory. This is not to suggest that everyone gets it right, or that it is always glorious in its expression. Not all wives come to me asking for my help in encouraging a husband toward greater leadership. Some come to me seeking refuge from a husband with despotic tendencies. But this too is a distortion of God's design and should be just as vigorously opposed as any other distortion.

I LOVE THAT MY HUSBAND LOVES IT HERE

The following is a true story.

A family began visiting our church after a difficult season of conflict in their home church. Eventually the scene disintegrated into a church split. Before long, they found the situation intolerable and visited "the church down the street." They were out kicking spiritual tires. As it was told to me, the pastor, beloved by this particular family, had been let go. Apparently the leadership dismissed the pastor because *she* was failing in her duties.

Needless to say, this family and our church had divergent views on the role of women within the church. As they would later discover, there were several theological convictions they disagreed with. The tradition of Calvinism to name one. But it was the gender issue that presented the biggest challenge. It took only a few weeks to figure this out. They had unwittingly joined a fellowship that held to a position that conflicted directly with a core conviction. In their minds, they had stepped back in time to some primitive age where wives called their husbands "lord" and walked three paces behind them. I think they stuck around for a few weeks to document their experience in the wild, like Jacques Cousteau.

The conflict was especially intense for the wife. She approached me after the service one day and put it out there. "I completely disagree with your position on women in the church and would like to talk to you about it." A few weeks later, we met.

When these types of conversations come along, I don't feel a need to win an argument or go on some theological rant. I enjoy the debate and discussion. In this case, I was truly interested in her perspective. In my tradition, it's not often a committed feminist visits your church. It's almost as rare as a unicorn running through the backyard. I was excited to meet with her. When we finally did meet, I was surprised by what transpired. She sat down and began.

"You know where I am on the issue of women in the church. Personally, I find your position insufferable and there's nothing you can say to convince me otherwise. But I've got a big problem on my hands. My husband loves this place. He finally feels as if he's in a church where he can connect. Actually, it's been awesome to see what's happening in his life and heart. He's beginning to lead the family in spiritual directions. I love it. He hasn't cared for spiritual things in so long. It's been a struggle to engage him. When I did, he would withdraw.

"Now he's bringing it up. He wants to talk about the Bible and pray with me. The other evening I woke up in the middle of the night to find his side of the bed empty. When I finally found him, he was in the study reading his Bible with tears in his eyes. When I sat down beside him, he held my hand and uttered one tearful statement: 'I'm sorry.'"

The smile on my face went all the way to my ears. I could not help it. She took note of it. "What's so funny?" But she knew already. This was the exact effect we've intended our ministry to have on men. We don't accept the cultural stereotype about men—namely, that we should set our expectations low. We have sought to create an environment where men feel the weight of their biblical responsibility and find compassionate help in taking it up. We've sought to recover the connection between masculinity and spirituality. Most men have never seen this done.

There is something very hopeful upon arriving at Community Bible Church and witnessing the unique blend of reformed teaching and humble masculinity. Most men thrive in the environment, as do their wives. This woman's husband was no exception. She was smiling back at me and acknowledging this in her own life. This committed egalitarian was flourishing under her husband's newfound desire for spiritual leadership within their home. Rather than objecting along philosophical lines, she was overjoyed as a wife. In her case, she had wanted her husband to lead, but her political leanings had not allowed her to ask. She assumed it would end in her oppression. But it did not. It ended in her joy.

THAT DEER-IN-THE-HEADLIGHTS LOOK

Most Christian husbands are clueless about what it means to lead their wives spiritually. How do I know? (Besides the fact that their wives tell me?) Because I ask them to define it pretty regularly. It's my job. You'd assume since they took on the responsibility in their wedding vows they would know what it entails. But they don't. When I ask, typically I'll get a deer-in-the-headlights look, or some homespun answer.

Ultimately, they're rattling off what they think I want to hear. Fundamentally, they overspiritualize it. They assume it means something it doesn't. For example, it does not mean they are required to be spiritual and intellectual giants. As if their vocabulary must be adjusted to include a certain number of *thees* and *thous*. Or that they have to speak in pietistic tones. Or wear clerical robes to dinner. As if being a spiritual leader means you sit around stroking your goatee uttering "Perhaps" at theological hypotheses. If this is what it means to be a spiritual leader, then it's easy to see why many men balk at the call to spiritual leadership. I'm out. But honestly, most wives get the definition of leadership wrong as well. They don't overspiritualize it as much as they romanticize it. It's fable-like. A knight-in-shining-armor kind of quality.

I was once counseling a couple struggling with the all-too-familiar issue of a husband's missing leadership. The wife had tried to explain her frustration, but he had no idea what she had been asking him to do. He "tried" everything. Her frustration only seemed to frustrate him. It's a very predictable cycle of misunderstanding. As we worked through the issues I asked her a rather obvious question: "What do you think spiritual leadership looks like?" As she answered, her husband rolled his eyes. I tried not to notice. What she ended up putting forth was characteristics that described a cross between an Old Testament prophet and a really awesome girlfriend. Her understanding was as skewed as his was.

Too often when I hear a wife describe what she's looking for in her husband she spends more time emphasizing what she doesn't like about him. It's more a confession of her deep disappointment with the man he turned out to be. What she wants is not a change in the husband she has, but a different version altogether. Sometimes the husband has been leading her spiritually, but she's been too preoccupied with some romanticized vision of masculinity to notice. Her point of reference is some idealized version of spiritual leadership, or her own personal preference, and not a definition that is biblical or informed by Christ.

Of course, this goes both ways. Husbands and wives alike can selfishly attempt to bend the disposition and tendencies of their mate to meet their personal needs and then justify their case using the Bible.

They may give their reasons in a spiritual overtone, but it's anything but. It's a blind kind of selfishness that binds fallen people to the preferences of their fickle hearts.

THE APRON AND THE BASIN

Fundamentally, spiritual leadership is service. In this way, it's not as we suppose. Too often we get this wrong.

Jesus had to correct this misunderstanding in the 12 disciples. They assumed that leadership meant power. In Christ it means weakness.

> Jesus called them to him and said, "You know that the rulers of the Gentiles lord it over them, and their great ones exercise authority over them. It shall not be so among you. But whoever would be great among you must be your servant, and whoever would be first among you must be your slave, even as the Son of Man came not to be served but to serve, and to give his life as a ransom for many" (Matthew 20:25-28).

In another place Christ said,

> At that time the disciples came to Jesus, saying, "Who is the greatest in the kingdom of heaven?" And calling to him a child, he put him in the midst of them and said, "Truly, I say to you, unless you turn and become like children, you will never enter the kingdom of heaven. Whoever humbles himself like this child is the greatest in the kingdom of heaven. Whoever receives one such child in my name receives me" (Matthew 18:1-5).

For a husband it translates into the humble, Christlike servant-mindedness of an imperfect man aimed at benefiting his imperfect wife. It's not about being a spiritual giant, a prolific reader, having an intensely theological mind, or being the equivalent of a walking thesaurus. It is not measured in the amount of biblical knowledge or the length of one's prayers.

Nor is it similar to the imbalances that run out in the other direction.

The ones that tend to layer the concept of leadership with bacon and dose it in English Leather. For the wife, it translates into an intense trust and forgiveness. Trust in that man whose trust is in God. Forgiveness in that man who will not lead her perfectly but desires to.

Leadership is about sacrifice. Practically, it is about living a sacrificial life on behalf of others. It is measured by the willingness of a man to sacrifice his personal needs for the needs of those under his care. Quite unexpectedly, then, being the spiritual leader of one's wife does not mean that you meet every expectation she has about how you should lead her, but that you lead her with unconditional love.

Furthermore, and maybe more importantly, it's not about a man checking boxes on a spiritual task list given to him by traditional perspectives, or his wife. There are plenty of men who never fail to read their Bibles yet never actually catch what's being communicated in what they read. A man who is gripped by the weight of his responsibility and realizes that he is carrying it out before an all-seeing God will lead from a place of deep sincerity.

Spirituality in a husband concerns his heart in relation to Jesus Christ and the gospel of grace. It comes down more to what constitutes the deepest passions of his life. More often than not, what impedes the spiritual leadership of a Christian husband is not the lack of passion, but a misplaced passion. He's passionate about stuff, money, or hobbies. He's a willing victim of domestic idols. It's a clear vision of Jesus that creates a sort of iconoclasm toward these secular images of happiness and rescues a man's heart from bondage to such ordinary things. It is Christ who makes a leader out of an idolater. A Christian husband who is a leader is first and foremost a worshipper of Jesus Christ. His greatest concern is not in pleasing his wife, but in pleasing his Lord. This pleases a wife.

IT'S NOT WHETHER BUT WHERE

I often tell husbands and fathers it's not *whether* they're leading, but *where*. Leadership is endowed to the husband by God as a spiritual law both in the marriage and family. Leadership happens whether they intended it to or not. Wherever their lives are headed, their family is headed. Whatever they value, their families will value. Whatever they love, their children will learn to love. It's a law of the soul.

If dad is into camping, they will camp. If dad is into doing nothing, they will do nothing. If dad is into entertainment, they will be easily bored. You cannot shake them. They will follow your life. If a dad reverses course and heads toward the things of God, it's likely he will hear the pitter-patter of little hearts following behind. It's the way God designed it. Consequently, then, when wives ask their husbands to lead, they're not really asking them to begin leading, but to change the direction of their leadership. Away from self and toward Christ.

A spiritual leader is not a confident man. Not in himself anyway. Not in his personal knowledge or ability. Self-confidence is too often what keeps men back from humble leadership. They are too proud to ask for help or admit defeat. A spiritual leader is a broken and weak man. He feels his inadequacy deeply and has a lower estimation of his abilities than anyone else under his care. He knows he is in over his head. He constantly depends on Christ's work and the Spirit's power.

A spiritual leader is always leading his wife to the cross of Christ and the gospel. Not back to a deeper confidence in himself. When a husband is broken over Christ's love for him on a deeply personal level, he is being more of a spiritual leader than at any other time. His affection spills out of his soul and into her life. It is this very devotion to Christ that makes him a better and more tender lover of his wife. It conforms him to the image of his Savior—namely, that of a servant.

I know Christian wives who have been praying for years that God would break into their husband's life and create a spiritual leader out of nothing. When I've had occasion I have asked the wife a question. "What have you been praying for?" "That he would be a spiritual leader, of course." When I press them for specifics, a pattern begins to emerge. "That he would be more thoughtful." "That he would pray with me." "That he would be less focused on his work." "That he would be more considerate of my needs." "That he would disciple the children."

All of these are appropriate in and of themselves, but they are more or less focused on peripheral matters or the needs of the wife. When they are presented as individual areas of improvement in a husband's leadership, they create a sort of bondage. The husband ends up with a list of tasks given to him by his wife comprised of various ways he can make her happy and improve their marriage. It leads to frustration all the way around because no human being can possibly do all that is necessary to maintain the happiness of any other human being.

This is why the divergent perspectives of "I don't know what else I can do to make her happy!" and "He doesn't seem to care about changing and improving our marriage!" show up in my office at the exact same time viewing the exact same set of facts. The wife continues to despair. The husband continues to withdraw.

But there is hope (for her) and freedom (for him). Both are found when wives desire the right thing for their husbands and for the right reason. A wife should not necessarily pray that her husband would do any specific thing, but that he would have a heart inclined toward one specific object—Jesus. "I pray that his love for Christ would overwhelm his life." As is consistently true in the Christian life, when the center is set, the margins are held in place also.

There may be no place this is more obvious than in marriage and a husband's leadership. She may "tell" him to do countless things, but what she really *needs* is for him to love Christ. In a mysterious way, consistent with the rest of Christianity, she does not need him to pay more attention to her, but to Christ and more desperately. This prayerful desire honors God, demonstrates respect for her husband, and keeps the focus off of self. But reciprocally, an increased devotion to the risen Lord in him results in an increased devotion to her. He becomes a man of graceful care because he is informed by Christ's graceful care of him. Godly marriages are primarily the result of the vertical relationship and not the horizontal one.

It is surprising how many wives lose sight of this simple truth. Or maybe it's not. After years of underwhelming leadership, their hopes languish. They will try anything to move the man who seems never to move. In their frustration, what husbands end up hearing is a litany of conditions set upon him by an unhappy wife. She wants him to speak more kindly to her. She needs him to be more appreciative of all she does. She would like him to help her with the kids. He needs to be more present in the marriage. All of this is reasonable, but it's not the problem.

My contention is that even if he did all of these things and more, he would not rise to the level of spiritual leader. He may do them in order to appease his wife and not because he loves her. This won't last. Furthermore, and unintentionally, the focus is on her and not Christ. But if this is ever reversed and the wife's central desire for her husband is his desire for Christ, changes inevitably begin to take place.

When God grips his heart, all the tedious little tasks of being a godly husband blend into one sincere act of brokenhearted service toward the wife. Not perfect, but real. What the wife needs in him is a change of heart toward Christ and not toward her.

No More Tips but Grace

I was in my office sitting across from an all-too-familiar scene. A couple—having run out of "tips for a happy marriage"—were before me trying not to strangle one another. No more niceties or weekend marriage seminars. They were on the brink and needed help. If Norman Rockwell had painted less nostalgic scenes and created more realistic ones, the one across from me would have shown up on the cover of a coffee-table book. The wife desperate and doing all the talking, the husband defeated and checking his watch, and the pastor listening intently past them to the root of the issue. At one point a classic exchange took place. "I don't want you traveling for work so much." "But I do what I do so you can have the life you want." Back and forth until her arms are crossed and his head is in his hands. The impasse.

Part of my job as counselor is to clarify the needle of truth in the haystack of these suburban messes. Marriages can get here. Most all do at some point whether we intend them to or not. We get jaded by years and routines and forget why we "fell in love" in the first place. We blink and the next thing we know we're divided by the common endeavor of life.

Despite all the finger pointing and anger, I could see what was happening. I had seen it before. The simple joy and freedom of the gospel had been lost on both of them. That image for marriage found in the cross of Christ with its basic truth—death to self brings joy in life— had been overshadowed by more complicated things. What I actually saw was a lonely wife, not an angry one. What she needed was *him*. His absence in her life brought on by the demands of life itself left a hole. One only he could fill. She actually understood why he worked and was grateful for it. It was an unavoidable tension. But this did not diminish her need for his presence in her life. She needed him. That was it. It was not the specifics, but him.

When I explained this to her, she looked at me as if I had read her mind. I asked, "Have you ever told him that you need him?" She said, "Why, no. I never thought to say that." "Well, tell him." She looked right at him with eyes full of tears. "Honey, I'm sorry I've frustrated you with all my criticisms. I've not known what to do. Up until this moment I did not know how to express what I was feeling. Truth is, I miss you and need you in my life. I can't function without the stability your presence provides. You've been my rock." He looked right back at her with tears in his eyes and said, "I totally get that. I'm sorry too."

You should be careful what you ask for. If you are praying that God would make a leader out of your husband, you might want to stop. I know this sounds contradictory (what wife doesn't want a spiritual leader?), but you should think through the implications first. What if God answered your prayers? What if he awakens your husband's heart and propels him into a passionate pursuit of His glory? Have you thought this through?

What if Christ seizes control of your husband's life and begins to dominate the horizon of his daily existence? It might not end where you think it will. Perhaps you're thinking he will focus more on you, but he will not. He will focus more on Christ. Obviously there will be an impact on his love and leadership of you, but the ultimate goal of his leadership will be Christ and not your personal happiness. In a real way, it will become less about what you want and more about what Christ would have for both of you. It will be less about suburban bliss and more about how the marriage and family proclaim the gospel to the surrounding community.

Think about it. If your husband should take the command given to husbands in Ephesians 5 seriously, his greatest concern for you will not be that you have everything you want, but that Christ be your greatest desire. After all, *your* devotion to Christ is *his* highest responsibility. It might mean that instead of cowering in fear as he normally does, he might confront your sin. He may call you to conformity to Christ in places you did not expect.

For certain it will mean your husband will fear Christ and not your reactions. He will weigh his decisions in light of Christ's glory and not your preference or his. What if he actually did take up the same responsibility in leadership of the kids? Can you imagine how disruptive this could prove? After all those years of bearing the responsibility yourself, how hard would it be for you to hand it over? What right does your husband have after he's been an absentee all these years? Seriously, it could get rough.

As Christ's supremacy rises in your husband's life, the priorities of his life will change. These changes can be extreme and sudden. I have seen husbands resolve to adjust their standard of living downward in order to live more generous lives. I've seen expensive cars sold, square footage downsized, and careers changed. All of this, obviously, impacts you directly.

It's not uncommon to see men decide to go into full-time ministry. It happens pretty frequently. After years spent squandering their spiritual lives or living as materialists, they quit their jobs, relocate their families across the country, and enter seminary. Or they go on short-term mission trips, which you encouraged, and upon returning home they announce they have been called to the mission field. In India, for instance. I've had more than one wife ask me to talk their husbands out such "craziness." Usually I don't. It's not crazy at all. In light of Christ, it makes sense. More often than not, I encourage it. "You went and got what you asked for, didn't ya?" I say.

THE SEVEN STAGES OF THE MARRIED COLD

*A husband's reactions to his wife's colds
during the first seven years of marriage*

First year: "Sugar dumpling, I'm really worried about my baby girl. You've got a bad sniffle, and there's no telling about these things with all the strep throat going around. I'm putting you in the hospital this afternoon for a general checkup, and a good rest."

Second year: "Listen, darling, I don't like the sound of that cough, and I've called Doc Miller to rush over here. Now you go to bed like a good girl, just for Poppa."

Third year: "Maybe you better lie down, honey. Nothing like a little rest when you feel lousy. I'll bring you something. Have we got any canned soup?"

Fourth year: "Now look, dear, be sensible. After you've fed the kids, and got the dishes done, and the floor finished, you better lie down."

Fifth year: "Why don't you take a couple of aspirin?"

Sixth year: "I wish you'd just gargle or something instead of sitting around barking like a seal all evening."

Seventh year: "For Pete's sake, stop sneezing! Are you trying to give me pneumonia?"

Then the LORD God said, "It is not good that the man should be alone; I will make him a helper fit for him." Now out of the ground the LORD God formed every beast of the field and every bird of the heavens and brought them to the man to see what he would call them. And whatever the man called every living creature, that was its name. The man gave names to all livestock and to the birds of the heavens and to every beast of the field. But for Adam there was not found a helper fit for him. So the LORD God caused a deep sleep to fall upon the man, and while he slept took one of his ribs and closed up its place with flesh. And the rib that the LORD God had taken from the man he made into a woman and brought her to the man. Then the man said, "This at last is bone of my bones and flesh of my flesh; she shall be called Woman, because she was taken out of Man." Therefore a man shall leave his father and his mother and hold fast to his wife, and they shall become one flesh. And the man and his wife were both naked and were not ashamed.

GENESIS 2:18-25

In Western culture today, you decide to get married because you feel a physical attraction to the other person. But a year or two later— or, just as often a month or two, three things usually happen. First, you begin to find out how selfish this wonderful person is. Second, you discover that this wonderful person has been going through a similar experience and he or she begins to tell you how selfish you are. And third, although you acknowledge it in part, you conclude that your spouse's selfishness is more problematic than your own.[10]

TIMOTHY KELLER, *THE MEANING OF MARRIAGE*

7

Marriage—Complex Problems Start from Simple Failures

I f you want to know what you truly believe about the gospel and the Christian life, you need look no further than your marriage. It is all there in living color. As in all places, the true measure of our Christian faith is not found in our ability to recite creeds, but to live them. We are most orthodox when we are most willing to ascend the crosses of self-denial made available to Christians in our relationships. And there is no relationship on earth where the grace of the gospel is more necessary than between husband and wife.

There is no purer proving ground of your love for the Savior than in the love you have for your husband. The fair gauge of our grasp of Christ is the ongoing attitude we show toward our spouse. I mean not merely the unsolicited kindnesses we offer when they least expect them—preparing a favorite meal, delivering coffee to a bedside. I mean more the many resentful acts and attitudes we resist doing when they most deserve them.

It's easy to be "filled with the Spirit" and gracious under the temporary field of view which friends and acquaintances have. We can all put on faces for those who see our lives one percent of the time. This is a natural and redundant sort of hypocrisy in which so many saints are all skilled. It's another thing altogether to live out your faith before that person you ride home with on Sunday afternoon following a particularly convicting sermon. We all know what it's like to be trapped in the silence of that ride with the one person who knows every reason

3

you should be repenting. It's one thing to step up and serve a neighbor or church member in need. It's another thing to constantly yield our rights to that one person who seems to be constantly demanding theirs. Your marriage is where the world pays closest attention to the continuity of your faith and practice. This is where the proof of a transformed life is most evident.

In this sense, marriage serves as the hard truth about who we are. Who we really are, that is. It is the most concrete application of humble self-sacrifice available to us in our Christian experience. It is the most enduring, intimate, personal, transparent relationship we have. Therefore, it requires the greatest measure of sacrifice of which we are capable. (Or not capable of actually.) It reveals finally what value we place on ourselves—servant or served. Or what value we place on others— servant or served. It makes clear how deeply we love Christ or grasp His love for us. It is where we learn whether the cross is a tattered cliché or a life-altering shift in the paradigm of human existence.

GETTING HONEST

Peer into your own marriage for a moment and ask some hard questions. You'll see what I mean. Is my love for my husband conditional? To be more specific, Do I place conditions on my love for him? It's tempting to answer no considering all you do for him in a given week. But the word *unconditional* stops us in our tracks. *Unconditional* goes beyond the fulfillment of duties and touches on the motive. It changes the question altogether.

Have there not been times you've resented him? Like when he's failed to offer a "Thank you" or acknowledge the numerous things you do for him? You know what I mean. When he just sits there as you fold laundry, or clean the kitchen after a meal. Come on. Of course you have. Do we not all immediately withhold kindness when we sense kindness has been withheld toward us? Of course we do. It's the default setting of the human heart. It's how we're wired. "I'll do what I'm supposed to do for you when you do what you are supposed to do for me." Or, "I'll fulfill my duties in this marriage when he fulfills his duties in this marriage."

When we unconditionally serve a person who does not deserve to be served, we are as near to what it means to follow Christ as we are capable of being. When we can say, "My love for my spouse is not conditioned upon his love for me," we are at the heart of God in His love toward us. When we mean this sincerely, the Spirit is fuller in us than at any other time. This self-sacrificing service toward undeserving sinners is the epicenter of redemption.

Understandably, it's hard to get the human heart up this slope. Like pushing a rope uphill. The gravity of our selfishness and self-righteousness constantly pulls us in the opposite direction. *Unconditional* is an impossibility for sinners. Without the Spirit of God filling us, we'll never muster the slightest ounce of it. As it is, the cross is the only place truly unconditional love has ever occurred. Without the event of the cross of Christ we've no reference point for true love at all or any hope for our marriage.

Not coincidentally, it's the failure to grasp the reality of unconditional love in the gospel which is at the root of troubled marriages. (It also goes missing in healthy ones.) When I sit with couples in crisis counseling and point out the vacancy here, the look on their faces is predictable. Like when a dog perks up his ears and turns his head in an inquiring way upon hearing a sound he can't quite figure out. Cross-focused love does that to self-absorbed people. It's unrecognizable. We come in thinking our marriages would be better if the other person would just do such and such. Or we would be happier if the other person would change in certain areas.

When you confront this tendency with the truth of the gospel, fuses have a tendency to blow. As a counselor, you realize you are swimming upstream against a narcissistic current that has been flowing since the Garden of Eden. "Why not be wronged?" or "Why not be defrauded?" is as foreign to our way of life as living underwater. Spouses come in pointing at each other since they (we) assume the problem *is* the other person. Like Adam and Eve, we're constantly tossing each other under the proverbial bus.

We always assume it's the other person because our end game is our pleasure and not the glory of Christ. If my starting point is my preference, then of course I'm always trying to bend people's behavior to accommodate me. I'm always assuming my happiness is the most essential reality. But if my starting point is the gospel, then it's my knees before God that are bent and not my mate's behavior.

Whatever they might be, the more complex problems in our relationships are always the result of fundamental failures. We must keep this in mind. Otherwise, we'll consistently repent of the wrong things without ever dealing with the *thing* beneath the *thing*. Or we'll look for quick fixes and not deal with the real problems.

I'm convinced that we want our issues to be more complex than they are. This way we can justify the extended self-focus, or blame our problems on people or circumstances. But they usually aren't complex at all. We needle at our souls in unending counseling sessions looking for some multifaceted feature of our issues until the search for "the root" becomes the reason we're in counseling to begin with. We are self-fulfilling prophecies in this way.

Truth is, the complex struggles arise from fundamental failures. Obviously they can be complicated, but not at their root. An affair—which has innumerable difficulties attached to it—resulted from a prideful discontentment in a man's soul, which itself arose from the idolatry of self. Idolatry is complex in nature but is a fundamental failure of worship. Furthermore, this failure—with all of its jagged edges—crept into the man's life over time as he failed to apprehend the basic construct of the cross and its implications in his own life and marriage. He did not just wake up one morning to find his shoes under some other woman's bed. He worshipped himself into that moment. When you get right down to it, that man did what he did because he was a self-focused idolater. The only reality that can break us from this tendency is grace.

WHAT WERE WE THINKING?

The naïveté of most engaged couples is stunning (and scary). They're clueless. Half the time I want to track down their parents and flog them. "What have you been doing for twenty years?" In my (Byron's) view, premarital counseling is for the purpose of talking two very naïve people out of marriage, not into it. One of them only wants to get the invitations out, and the other wants to get to the honeymoon. Each of them possess a view of marriage that barely extends beyond guest lists or wedding receptions. But to their surprise, premarital counseling is not merely about providing information on basic issues within marriage such as communication, finances, sex, etc. It includes all this, but is not limited to it. If it is limited to these more functional aspects then we have failed to actually counsel about marriage. Premarital counseling should serve as a final warning for two very selfish and ignorant sinners. A warning not only about their future spouse's flaws, but their own as well.

Premarital sessions with me can get intense. It's all part of my strategy. Most couples approach these sessions like they do an annual checkup at the dentist—a necessary evil. It's perfunctory in nature. They come in expecting to get their card punched. Instead, they get punched. Right in the "get a clue" region of their brain. More than once, following the first session, a couple has cancelled on me. "You're too intense," is what I generally hear. And they would be right. But if they can survive me, they should get married.

Fact is, my challenges to their idealized visions of marriage are nothing compared to the challenges marriage itself provides. The way I see it, you can deal with it now, or you deal with it ten years from now. In a real sense, all marital counseling is premarital counseling. A decade into marriage when a couple sits before me, we're merely going back and restating what they failed to hear in the beginning.

In premarital, once you start laying out the shortcomings in their relationship or the struggles with the individuals themselves, they start to panic. Especially the bride. All they hear is an explanation of why they should call the ceremony off. But my message is not "You shouldn't be getting married." My message is "Be honest with yourself and each other before heading toward marriage. This way, you'll resist the impulse to walk away from marriage when things get tough."

I tell them, "Here's what you are going to face ten years from now. Here is where you are going to need grace to deal with each other. Here is what is going to make him hard to follow. Here is what's going to make her hard to lead. Here is why your marriage must rest on the gospel and be viewed through the spectrum of the cross." This is not to suggest that marriage is drudgery or without joy. Rather, it is to argue that true freedom and joy within marriage come from a rather radical reversal of perspective. A frame of mind dominated by that one overwhelming word *unconditional*.

Over the years, I have stood with countless couples at the altar. Two sinners and an officiant (no less a sinner) transacting covenant vows before a holy God. More than once, prior to the exchange of vows, I've looked straight at that sweet couple and declared something along these lines:

> The world would tell you to find someone who can make you happy and marry that person. They would have you believe this formula works. But this is a self-inflicted bondage and a path that leads away from contentment and not near it as we have supposed. To hang our contentment or peace of mind on the performance of another human being is futile. No one can make you happy. People disappoint. Even those who vow they never will. To live this way is to live for self and selfishly. It does not result in love, but cruelty. It is not a means to happiness, but most often the very reason happiness fails to exist in so many marriages. It is also a subtle denial of all the vows you are about to make.

> The gospel beckons you in an opposite direction. It does not say, "Find someone who you can be happy with, or that you find attractive," but "Find someone you can serve and serve with." It asks us to bind ourselves to a fallen and imperfect human being and love them with the type of love with which you have been loved. Happiness comes not by making happiness the goal of your marriage, but the glory of God.

THE CHARGE TO THE WIFE

[Give] thanks always and for everything to God the Father in the name of our Lord Jesus Christ, submitting to one another out of reverence for Christ. Wives, submit to your own husbands, as to the Lord. For the husband is the head of the wife even as Christ is the head of the church, his body, and is himself its Savior. Now as the church submits to Christ, so also wives should submit in everything to their husbands (Ephesians 5:20-24).

We typically approach this passage as a series of tips to a better marriage. It's more along the lines of a reality check. This is where the rubber of the gospel meets the road of life in the epistle to the Ephesians. There's a definite flow to the argument that finally arrives at the wedding day. There is a reason marriage shows up at this point in the apostle's letter. Having so clearly demonstrated the glories of the gospel of Christ (chapters 1–3) Paul then moves on to reveal its power in the here and now (chapters 4–6). All that has been accomplished (redemption and reconciliation) flows down to the contours of the human experience—into relationships. All of those glorious truths of grace found in the anthem of Ephesians 1 trickle down to the details of human existence in Ephesians 5.

It's as if Paul began in the stratosphere of eternity past and traced the thread of redemption from the macro level through time and space right down into the micro level of the relationships between husband and wife. This is where the principles Paul has just articulated find their primary application. From this we realize that all we are called to do as husband and wife ultimately results from realizing what God has done for us in Christ.

What we've been called to in marriage as Christians makes no sense unless we start in the stratosphere of grace. It is the divine "illogic" of the cross that makes it make sense. The view from atop Calvary is so contrary to the world's. The world would encourage doing what's best for us. Standing up for our rights. But our petty little battles for us seem so ridiculous under the shadow of a dying Savior.

In God's economy there is no demanding of rights, no priority of our needs over those of others. There is only a dying to self and a yielding of our rights. This, of course, makes no sense until we understand that our Savior walked this very path in redemption. In ways that will always remain a mystery to us, the greatest power ever exerted on earth was in that act which was the lowliest. Herein lies the mysterious power of marriage—when we yield instead of demand, we find the blessings that have always eluded us. Always.

> Then Jesus said to His disciples, "If anyone would come after me, let him deny himself and take up his cross and follow me. For whoever would save his life will lose it; but whoever loses his life for my sake *will find it*" (Matthew 16:24-25, emphasis added).

THE DREADED "S" WORD

> Wives, submit to your own husbands, *as to the Lord* (Ephesians 5:22, emphasis added).

The responsibilities of husband and wife may manifest themselves differently within the marriage, but both husband and wife end up in the same place—under the shadow of the cross. For certain there is an order in marriage that God has ordained. One follows. The other leads. But neither is greater than the other. The gospel forbids such conclusions: "There is neither Jew nor Greek, there is neither slave nor free, there is no male and female; for you are all one in Christ Jesus" (Galatians 3:28).

The issue presented in this passage does not concern the presence of order or authority. Paul is not denying the distinctions between males and females. The distinctions do exist. The issue in this passage is a question of one's merit before God. Whether male or female, sinners come to God on the same basis—mercy. There are males and females and a certain structure assumed within the marriage relationship. But both male and female stand before God in a righteousness that is not their own and by a grace that comes from God. When it comes to grace, there is neither male nor female. There is only grace.

The nature of authority within Christian marriage is not a matter of supremacy or power. It is one of self-subordination. In every other context besides Christianity, authority is about rule and power. In these places, authority becomes something by which to measure success. A superior status. But under the reign of the gospel, authority relegates one to the lowest available position in a culture—a servant. In Christianity, power is about service. In the mystery of the gospel, neither the one possessing authority or the one submitting to it is any less the servant of the other. He who has the power is under the bondage of service to the one who doesn't. But neither party is any less the beneficiary of the other's service.

This is why Christ's sacrificial life is the model for both husband and wife. The wife models the humble surrender of the selfless Son of God. The husband models the boundless self-sacrifice of the Savior. There is here found an endless symmetry of graceful service. The primary objective of the husband's authority is the care of his wife. As he seeks to protect and serve her, she is drawn up under the shelter of his care, not repelled by it. As she does, he is encouraged to serve her all the more. This love goes round and round this way, pulling itself along until questions about who's in charge are overshadowed by the servitude of both.

A PESKY LITTLE CLAUSE

As a wife, yours is the most challenging of the roles within a marriage. This is because it requires a more delicate and deeper grace. You are called of God to follow an imperfect leader. Entrusting your life to a fallen creature complete with obvious imperfections is a great adventure in faith. He is inadequate on every level. The sensation of this in your life must be similar to that of a student driving instructor who hands over the keys and places his life in the hands of an unproven and distracted adolescent. How you are able to resist reaching for the wheel is beyond me. Obviously, many wives do. Some never let go. The view from the passenger seat requires an abundant faith.

By far, the most difficult part of your task is letting your husband fail while simultaneously retaining a trust in the sovereignty of God and respect for your husband. There is a natural apprehension in many wives that her husband will fail in his obligations and jeopardize the well-being of the family. Driven by this concern, and because of the husband's negligence, the wife may take up an unnatural position of leadership just to keep the whole thing afloat. The wife then gets caught in this vicious cycle of having a godly desire for her husband to lead, but having to take up leadership out of fear. She ends up becoming the de facto leader of the home. And as many wives can tell you, once you get the keys, it's hard to ever give them back.

I (Byron) will let you in on something. We husbands know our wives are more competent than we are. This is part of the reason we are so insecure and often dismiss your suggestions with belittling barks. Our pride won't let us turn to your advice. Our insecurity comes out in slights and insults. How you put up with this nonsense is beyond me. To survive here, you must look to something beyond the limited stature of your husband.

For certain, if your sense of security is derived from the consistency of your husband's life, you're destined for frustration. Reciprocally, if his sense of peace is dependent on you, he will share your fate. This is precisely where Christ comes in. To love your husband as you should, you have to look beyond him to Calvary. Ultimately, this is what Paul was getting at.

This pesky little clause "as to the Lord" directed at the wife in Ephesians 5:22 changes everything. (The same way "as Christ does for the church" does for the husband.) It distinguishes the Christian view of marriage from every other view. It brings the duty of the wife into the arena of the heart. It means your responsibility is not conditioned on the quality of your husband's love for you (which is flawed), but on Christ's (which is perfect). It is not about your husband's worth, his personal character, or relative abilities as a leader.

You are not called to serve your husband only if he is a spiritual giant. Or when he is doing everything right. Or when he is obedient to the Word of God. Or when he deserves your service. Or only if he is a believer. Or only if you deem him worthy at any given point. There is no condition here. There is no "unless" clause in all of this because any such conditions are always met with Christ.

It also means it's not enough to go through the motions. It's a matter of the heart. You cannot say, "I'll do it, but I'm not going to enjoy it." It's not done begrudgingly. You cannot make your husband pay for it as you do it.

> …let it be the hidden person of the heart, with the imperishable quality of a gentle and quiet spirit, which is precious in the sight of God (1 Peter 3:4).

It means that your submission to your husband is a reflection of your devotion to Christ. Because you are obeying God's design as you are obeying Christ, your willingness to submit yourself to your husband's leadership is a demonstration of your devotion to Christ. If your devotion to Christ is shallow and superficial, so will be your commitment to your role in the marriage.

This means you are never alone. If you have little or no relationship with your husband, you must be able to fall back on your relationship with your Lord. You have to constantly be looking over the shoulder of your husband to the cross of Christ.

A "WHY" WE WERE NOT EXPECTING

> For the husband is the head of the wife even as Christ is the head of the church, his body, and is himself its Savior. Now as the church submits to Christ, so also wives should submit in everything to their husbands (Ephesians 5:23-24).

"Why do I have to surrender my life?" There are a number of things the apostle could have said to satisfy this question. He could have been heavy-handed and said, "Because God said so." He could have been fatalistic: "Because that's the way things are." He could have been sanc-timonious: "Because it's right." Instead, he was gracious and hopeful: "Because it's the best thing." This question receives a simple answer: Because God has designed it this way, and in His design there is great wisdom. The point of Paul's words is to bring out the benefit of God's design, not the cruelty of it.

The point is not that the wife is any less essential or able. The point is that the design has purpose. The parallel is found in the analogy that says Christ is the head of the church. That is an essential relationship. True joy comes from understanding and trusting in that design. It is the way God cares for you. It is the way God protects you. It is the way God fulfills you. It is the way God uses you. It is the way God benefits you. It is the way God loves you. It is the way God provides for you. You may be thinking to yourself, *How is that possible?* Just keep in mind God is in the business of using imperfect instruments to fulfill His purposes.

NOW—WADE, LAUREN, AND BLAKE
AGES THIRTEEN, SIXTEEN, AND TEN

A HUSBAND'S COMMUNICATION SAFETY GUIDE

. Men know there are days when all they have to do is open their mouth and they are taking their own life into their hands. This is a guide that should be as common as a driver's license in the wallet of every husband. Each discussion and response is ranked in order of personal safety.

Subject One: Clothing

> Dangerous: Are you wearing that?
> Safer: Wow, you look good in brown.
> Safest: Wow! Look at you!
> Ultrasafe: Have some chocolate.

Subject Two: Emotions

> Dangerous: What are you so worked up about?
> Safer: Could we be overreacting?
> Safest: Here's my paycheck.
> Ultrasafe: Have some chocolate.

Subject Three: Duties

> Dangerous: What did you do all day?
> Safer: I hope you didn't overdo it today.
> Safest: I have always loved you in that robe!
> Ultrasafe: Have some chocolate.

Cleanliness is next to godliness.
No One Ever

Now as they went on their way, Jesus entered a village. And a woman named Martha welcomed him into her house. And she had a sister called Mary, who sat at the Lord's feet and listened to his teaching. But Martha was distracted with much serving. And she went up to him and said, "Lord, do you not care that my sister has left me to serve alone? Tell her then to help me." But the Lord answered her, "Martha, Martha, you are anxious and troubled about many things, but one thing is necessary. Mary has chosen the good portion, which will not be taken away from her."

Luke 10:38-42

8

FREEDOM—NEVER FEAR
ANSWERING THE DOOR

I (Robin) was part of a support group for seminary wives offered by my husband's alma mater. It was our first semester, and I was all in. The meetings were designed to serve as a weekly "you're not crazy" session for the young wives and moms whose husbands were in the throes of ministry education. The transition from civilian to seminary life can be jarring. Essentially, you and your husband mutually agree it best to separate for three to four years as he disappears into endless reports and tests while you man the wheel of the family. All for the kingdom of God, of course. It does not take long for the reality of this decision to set in. It can be a lonely season. Obviously it's all worth it, but around week three you begin to wonder what you were thinking. It is no easy task.

When Byron graduated and walked across the stage to receive his diploma, I kept thinking about how the school should have a separate graduation for seminary wives. No doubt I earned a degree somewhere in something. Instead of diplomas, they would hand out spa treatments and cruises to the northern Caribbean. Yeah, that would work. Of course, that never happened. But I've never regretted a minute of the time I spent making sure he was prepared for our ministry together. Gospel ministry has been worth every moment he spent buried in some giant book or was pronouncing unrecognizable Hebrew or Greek letters to himself.

The support group meetings had two features—a lecture, followed by discussion. The lecturer was usually the wife of a pastor or professor.

Typically the topics were big doses of encouragement being offered by women who had survived what we were in the middle of trying to survive ourselves. It was Seminary Wives Anonymous. The discussion groups were invaluable. We'd respond to the lecture and open our hearts up in front of each other, seeking to encourage or be encouraged ourselves. Real friendships were forged here. Some of the other women remain my closest of friends to this day. The messages seemed to always be just what I needed to hear at the time. Well, almost all of them anyway.

On one particular evening I had settled into my spot along with my small group members and discussion leader. The topic on this given evening was "Keeping Your Home," or something along those lines. I cannot remember the specific title of the lecture, but the lecture itself is burned into my database. After some preliminaries about schedules, calendars, charts, and routines the kind lady behind the microphone said something that landed on me like a ton of bricks.

> Let's say someone decides to come by your home unannounced in the middle of the day. If when they knock on your door your first instinct is to start cleaning up and shoving stuff in closets before you answer the door, you're failing as a housekeeper. Your house should always be prepared for the unexpected visitor. Your home should be prepared. This is all part of entertaining and your responsibility as a pastor's wife.

I instinctually laughed. To this day I do not know if I laughed out loud. What I was thinking to myself at the time was, *If someone stops by unannounced and knocks on my door I'm cutting off the lights and pretending I'm not home.* Honestly, my worst fear is someone stopping over unannounced. Then I realized she was serious. I froze. I didn't move for a few minutes. I didn't want anyone to see the shock on my face. If I reacted, the ladies around me might notice. I would be ousted as a bad wife and homemaker. An unfit pastor's wife. My husband's ministry would be over before it began. There may be no more horrifying reality for a wife than being labeled as that woman who keeps an untidy or messy home. "Bad homemaker" is the kiss of death when it comes to domestic respectability.

All I could think about was the pile of unfolded laundry sitting in my living room at that very moment. It was mocking me. That wicked pile of laundry has followed me everywhere I've been. It's always there, never allowing me to finish my work around the house. It's my nemesis. I'm never quite done. The lecture went on to measure out the standards of good housekeeping. The speaker went on to offer all kinds of tips. "If you run the vacuum cleaner for a few minutes before he gets home, he will think you have been cleaning all day." Priceless. When the small group commenced, I assumed I was the only one who found the lecture unnerving. As a new member of the group, I was naïvely wondering at everyone else's ability to pull all this off. But there was not much talking when the lecture was over. As it turned out, I was not the only one reeling.

A Suffocating Standard

At first take, the speaker's advice may sound wise and insightful, but it's actually awful. Think about the implications of her admonition for a moment. *There should never be a time that your home is not put together.* Really? That's impossible. Fact is there are times—some more often than others—when life invades our good intentions or best efforts. When our schedules are interrupted by domestic invaders like vomit, the flu, or a three-year-old with diarrhea. Regardless of what the speaker intended, she should know wives and mothers have a tendency to hear her counsel differently. Here's how we're prone to translate it: *You should always be concerned about someone discovering that you are a flawed human being.*

The Insane Pressure of Performance

That is the very thing we women live our lives avoiding. This is the last type of counsel we need to hear. Fundamentally, what she asked us to do was measure ourselves against our relative ability to perform a duty and not Christ's perfect righteousness, which had secured our standing before God. This kind of denial is subtle but it seems always to linger around a view of womanhood. The irrational fear of perception is our default mode of operation. There is a pressure of conformity to some assumed domestic standard always resting on our lives. No one wants to admit it's there, but this strain is the worst-kept secret among women.

We do it with everything. We're always leaning more toward Martha than we are toward Mary. Take new moms, for example. Regardless of how many times they've read *What to Expect When You're Expecting*, they will never expect what's actually coming. Despite the odds, they assume they will be the exception when it comes to caring for an infant. They expect to master nursing, or reflux, or sleep schedules on the very first try. Hours after arriving home with the bundle of joy, they begin to realize the truth. They are no exception.

The experience of that first baby is hard. She and her husband have no clue what they are doing. Who thought it was a good idea to send them home with another human being who was completely dependent on them anyway? Exhausted and frustrated, she breaks down in tears. The husband is doing laps in the car hoping the ride will put the "little bundle" to sleep. First thing that comes to her mind? I'm a bad mother. What's more, there are countless experienced mothers out there who would be more than willing to offer help and counsel, but they won't reach out. And why not? Because she's expected to be a good mom. She has to do this on her own. In her mind, asking for help would be admitting defeat.

Women can suffer unrelentingly under this sort of suffocating standard. Appearance. Children. Homes. Do our husbands suffer the same way? Uh, not so much. For us it's both self-imposed and cultural. Our moms set the standard on us, and we pay it forward by setting it on our daughters. This is especially true for Christian women.

Ultimately, the church may be the worst purveyors of this type of insanity. This is because so much of a Christian view of wives and moms comes down to duties. Most of the teaching for women centers on performing the domestic duties given to women by God. Too often the sum total of this teaching doesn't rise far above a sanctified course in home economics. Our standard lies somewhere between the Proverbs 31 woman and a Stepford Wife.

But it does not stop here. We hold others captive to this tendency by using their approval as a measure of self-worth. For certain, so much of what we do is done in order to gain the approval of others. How many women have tried for years to gain the approval of their moms through their families and children? But we can do this with everyone. Our reward becomes the recognition by others that we have done a good job. It's no longer about the sincerity of service before God. If someone fails to thank us or draw attention to our performance, we feel slighted or discouraged. This not only enslaves us but others as we indirectly force them to applaud our efforts.

Now don't get me wrong: I have my standards. I'm a scheduling freak of sorts. My children could share some mommy dearest moments with you. I have my own "no wire hangers" type of issues. So this argument should not be understood as a license to neglect our responsibilities as Christian wives and mothers. There are those ladies who always seem to make their families and children sound like burdens. Our husbands and families are our ministry. So the problem in this is not an emphasis on the duties that God has ordained, but the lack of emphasis on the grace necessary to fulfill them. We seem to only preach duty to wives and never preach the gospel that ultimately makes the duties make sense.

Christian women too often mistake cleanliness, neatness, and orderliness for godliness. But, fact is, you can have a spotless home as a Christian woman and be nowhere nearer to pleasing God. In the same way, it's possible to never say anything or do anything disrespectful toward your husband yet still have little or no respect for him. Point is, women more than men can get comfortable with superficial displays of righteousness because so much of their spirituality is measured in tasks. We can take comfort in appearances.

If we're not careful, what people think of our spiritual lives can surpass the actual quality of our spiritual lives. Getting a Bible study done on time for the weekly women's group at church becomes more important than benefiting from the study itself. Serving in the children's ministry is more about checking a box of service than helping propagate the gospel through ministry to children. As the episode of Martha demonstrates, being busy is not a spiritual virtue.

> Now as they went on their way, Jesus entered a village. And a woman named Martha welcomed him into her house. And she had a sister called Mary, who sat at the Lord's feet and listened to his teaching. But Martha was distracted with much serving. And she went up to him and said, "Lord, do you not care that my sister has left me to serve alone? Tell her then to help me." But the Lord answered her, "Martha, Martha, you are anxious and troubled about many things, but one thing is necessary. Mary has chosen the good portion, which will not be taken away from her" (Luke 10:38-42).

Without exception, all of us (both men and women) trend toward performance in our Christian lives. But women seem to be better at it. Jesus strongly cautioned against getting godliness and activities confused:

> Beware of practicing your righteousness before other people in order to be seen by them, for then you will have no reward from your Father who is in heaven (Matthew 6:1).

Women—more than any others in the church—are susceptible to practicing their righteous deeds before men in the very way Jesus warned against. We care far too much of perception and what people think of us. Correspondingly, we more than most need to know and understand the freedom that the gospel provides from such bondage. Unfortunately, this is usually not the message we hear. Our teaching on womanhood is nearly completely absent of the gospel of grace. It is nearly exclusively committed to law and not grace. Christian womanhood as propagated by evangelicalism is too often reduced down to one extensive and unending to-do list.

Almost all of our emphasis boils down to a feminized brand of moralism. A notable example is the common use of the Proverbs 31 woman as a template for feminine godliness and self-discipline. Without hesitation we assume the point of Proverb 31 is to offer a pattern of behavior. To question this interpretation is sacrilege. Think of all the Christian coffee mugs and Thomas Kinkade-like prints that bear this emphasis. The assumption is rampant. But is this really the point? For certain we can learn from the woman described in Proverbs 31. But patterning our lives after a fallen human being (even one found in the Bible) is in direct contradiction to the point of the Bible itself—"for all have sinned and fall short of the glory of God" (Romans 3:23). I think many of us have taken what was a poem composed by a doting husband and turned it into a behavioral strategy for godliness.

LIFE IN THE FISHBOWL OF PERFECTION

As a pastor's wife, the pressure on me to perform is compounded by my husband's public life. I'll confess that I do worry what people think of me, our kids, and our family. I'm constantly aware that we're under the public eye. I think we're supposed to appear to others as that family that comes in the frame. But as my husband is prone to say, there is no such family. What's striking to me is the distance between the perceived ideal of a pastor's family and who we actually are as people. We're a normal family. That is to say, we are ordinary, broken-down people in constant need of God's grace. My husband is not perfect. My kids are not perfect. I'm nowhere near perfect. Inevitably there are some who expect us to be. Of course, in reality I may be the only one laying this expectation on me. But either way, the pressure is always there.

What has constantly relieved me of this burden is the incessant declaration and explanation of the gospel in our home and through my husband's ministry. As a family, we try never to assume it. We also never assume we're not assuming it. Since I have a tendency to beat myself up over my failures and imperfections as a mother and wife, the message of grace seems always to be restoring my soul. Despite all my many sins, I am righteous before God due to Christ's perfect righteousness.

This thought constantly astonishes me. Especially as I look at the ever-present pile of laundry and my many unfinished duties. God's love for me is not contingent on the performance of my duties. This thought liberates me and restores the joy of my service. When I am overwhelmed or have fallen short in attitude and duty, it keeps me from reaching for the "bootstraps" of effort. It is done. God is pleased with me even when I am not pleased with myself. My husband recently wrote of this reality in another place:

> If the problem with Christian men in the modern evangelical church is a tolerance of their failure to act as men, then the corresponding problem on the other side is the exact opposite—our intolerance of any perceived failure in our Christian women. Our men are in bondage to an extended adolescence that the church has proliferated through low expectations. Our women are in bondage to a form of perfectionism that the church has encouraged through unrealistic expectations. The contrast in what we have come to expect from the genders could not be more stark. The similarity here, however, is also stark—the inability of the church to apply the gospel as the remedy in both extremes.
>
> The recent call within evangelicalism for men to abandon their negligence has been well and good. There are signs of great progress. The gospel has begun to take center stage, as well as take root in many hearts. Men have been motivated by the spectacle of grace to *take up* their responsibility and lead. But where is the corresponding call on our women to *lay down* the burden of performance set on them by the good intentions of the church? Who is calling our women with equal zeal out of their own peculiar bondage to the same grace of Christ? While setting our men free from one prison, have we abandoned our women to languish in another?
>
> If there is one creature in the church of Christ that silently struggles under the weight of works righteousness, it has to be the wife and mother. The alchemy for hypocrisy

found within her Christian duty is greater than most others. Wives and moms can easily keep the true condition of their hearts from view behind unending tasks and domestic responsibilities. The calls to submission and a quiet spirit may well be interpreted by them as prohibitions against any failure or personal weakness. And that is tragic. Women are expected to have it all together. Mechanical, burdensome, and joyless womanhood can drone on if we forget that one thing which rises above all our duties and gives them meaning—Jesus Christ.[11]

In this, and many other similar ways, we have robbed women within the church of the sincere joy of Christian womanhood. We have kept them back from grace and true freedom. Godliness comes from a relationship with Christ Jesus and a transformed heart, not a to-do list.

To be clear, the aim is not to be liberated from one's responsibilities, to excuse neglect, or deny God's design of male authority. The aim is to be liberated from the tendency to measure ourselves by our performance in fulfilling the duties we are called to. Our righteousness is outside of us in Christ and not in our relative ability to keep a clean house. It is this latter awareness that liberates us to undertake our duty with complete joy and freedom.

WHEN JESUS BECOMES CLUTTER

It is the account of a woman anointing Jesus' feet that reorients my focus. This broken woman is the antidote to the Martha hiding inside me. Her extravagant devotion puts my performance-based religion in its place. She reminds me of what it means to love and adore Jesus.

What's most obvious to me about this woman is how unacceptable her behavior is to what's typically accepted among Christian women. No woman in her right mind would do what she did. I can only imagine how uncomfortable she made everyone in attendance. This would have been shocking behavior. This was unsuitable for church and disruptive to the extreme.

She stepped on a number of key taboos and traditions to get to

Jesus. This type of display would have been highly controversial for anyone to carry out, but for a woman to do it pushed the whole scene over the top. It was beyond scandalous. Not surprisingly, it angered even the disciples.

> When the disciples saw it, they were indignant, saying, "Why this waste? For this [perfume] could have been sold for a large sum and given to the poor" (Matthew 26:8-9).

Yet the disciples completely missed it. They had been missing it for months. But it had been there the entire time. So close, yet so far. The disciples are me. I miss it. At this moment, they were upset about meeting all the expenses associated with Jesus' ministry and forgot Jesus' true mission in the process. But the woman (along with countless other atypical characters in the Bible) did not miss it. She got it. And in the biggest way.

"Waste" is the dominant word in this passage. It leaps off the page. A simple symbol can sum up the entirety of our perspective. One person's waste is another person's worship. I suppose it all depends on the one on whom you're wasting it. What the disciples saw as waste she considered an inadequate sacrifice. They were unwilling to go to such lengths to demonstrate their love and gratitude for Christ. It was beneath them. Without realizing it, their rebuke revealed their true estimation of Jesus Christ. Without realizing it, our lack of brokenness around Jesus reveals ours. When Jesus rebukes the disciples, He's rebuking us.

> Jesus, aware of this, said to them, "Why do you trouble the woman? For she has done a beautiful thing to me. For you always have the poor with you, but will not always have me" (verses 10-11).

Not surprisingly, the very behavior that offended everyone else in attendance pleased Jesus. What they saw as careless Jesus called "good." We always get it backwards. According to Jesus, her level of sacrifice and devotion was appropriate. That is to say, it was appropriately scandalous. All this time with Jesus, these men had failed to see Him for who

He was. He had been telling them all along what He came to do for them, but it never occurred to them to worship Him for it.

> Then he strictly charged the disciples to tell no one that he was the Christ. From that time Jesus began to show his disciples that he must go to Jerusalem and suffer many things from the elders and chief priests and scribes, and be killed, and on the third day be raised. And Peter took him aside and began to rebuke him, saying, "Far be it from you, Lord! This shall never happen to you" (Matthew 16:20-22).

Jesus was clutter. That's me. I have forgotten to worship my Savior. I too have failed to kiss the feet of the One who gave Himself for me. This type of adoration was above me. Fundamentally, what I came to realize is that there's no way to overstate sincere adoration of the person and work of Christ. That's impossible. What is more than possible is to forget to do it at all.

THE GOOD WIFE'S GUIDE

(Source unknown, allegedly from the 1950s)

- Have dinner ready. Plan ahead, even the night before, to have a delicious meal ready on time for his return. This is a way of letting him know that you have been thinking about him and are concerned about his needs. Most men are hungry when they get home and the prospect of a good meal is part of the warm welcome needed.

- Prepare yourself. Take 15 minutes to rest so you'll be refreshed when he arrives. Touch up your makeup, put a ribbon in your hair and be fresh-looking. He has just been with a lot of work-weary people.

- Be a little gay and a little more interesting for him. His boring day may need a lift and one of your duties is to provide it.

- Clear away the clutter. Make one last trip through the main part of the house just before your husband arrives. Run a dustcloth over the tables.

- During the cooler months of the year you should prepare and light a fire for him to unwind by. Your husband will feel he has reached a haven of rest and order, and it will give you a lift too. After all, catering to his comfort will provide you with immense personal satisfaction.

- Minimize all noise. At the time of his arrival, eliminate all noise of the washer, dryer or vacuum. Encourage the children to be quiet.

- Be happy to see him.

- Greet him with a warm smile and show sincerity in your desire to please him.

- Listen to him. You may have a dozen important things to tell him, but the moment of his arrival is not the time. Let him talk first—remember, his topics of conversation are more important than yours.

- Don't greet him with complaints and problems.
- Don't complain if he's late for dinner or even if he stays out all night. Count this as minor compared to what he might have gone through at work.
- Make him comfortable. Have him lean back in a comfortable chair or lie him down in the bedroom. Have a cool or warm drink ready for him.
- Arrange his pillow and offer to take off his shoes. Speak in a low, soothing and pleasant voice.
- Don't ask him questions about his actions or question his judgment or integrity. Remember, he is the master of the house and as such will always exercise his will with fairness and truthfulness. You have no right to question him.
- A good wife always knows her place.[12]

"I now know my appearance, guys, and
professional success don't provide
lasting security. If I put all my hope in
them, I'm bound to be disappointed.
Christ alone will never fail me…"

LAUREN SCRUGGS

The American Association of Plastic Surgeons reported
that there were 11.7 million cosmetic surgeries performed
in America in 2007. Humanity is obsessed with
appearance… This is a frightening reality, because the
Lord sees each sinful and selfish desire of our heart.[13]

PAUL TRIPP

Charm is deceitful and beauty is vain, but a woman
who fears the LORD is to be praised. Give her the fruit of
her hands, and let her works praise her in the gates.

PROVERBS 31:30-31

9

Beauty—You Are Beautiful

I (Byron) can't imagine the pressure women suffer regarding their self-image. The demands set on women (young and old) by the culture to be thin, beautiful, fashionably up-to-date, and flawless is relentless. It must be unbearable. Honestly, I wouldn't know. I'm a middle-aged man who frequently horrifies my children by my wardrobe choices. It's a dad's duty to embarrass his kids by not really caring. I live in a different world than my wife, where black socks and sandals are part of the uniform. I guess I'm from Venus after all. It takes me less than ten minutes to shower and dress. Not so with my bride. My wife and I come home from a late night out with friends and I can brush my teeth, fall into bed, and be asleep in three minutes. Not so with my bride. She cries "Foul!" all the time on this one. This no doubt explains why she seems to do cannonballs while getting into bed from time to time. "Oh, I'm sorry. Were you asleep?"

If you think about it, you'll agree there is a disproportionate sort of low expectation set on our young men as compared to our young ladies. It seems we expect very little of them. It also seems they have no problem complying. But our women must be perfect.

Every second, images of mythological beauty are contrasted with their own fragile self-image. Photoshopped illusions mock them as they stand in front of mirrors assessing the damage of their genetic hand-me-downs. If they are not put together just right, we assume something is wrong with them. It's an impossible standard. They know all too well that they are flawed. It's a losing battle. We're all flawed. No one is perfect, and we all know this.

133

Nonetheless, we seem idolatrously fixed on this message emanating from our culture—"Be attractive, and you will be valued." As a result, young women who can't possibly comply end up feeling undervalued, or worse, unloved. Some go to heartbreaking lengths to cope with the stress and garner affection.

Eating disorders, injuring themselves, and sometimes taking their own life. It seems no woman is exempt. Even those women whom other women would consider specimens of physical beauty struggle with the myth of perfectionism and body image problems. They too are more than able at identifying their numerous flaws. It's narcissistic insanity.

THE BROMIDES OF A RANTING FATHER

Dear old dad has been emitting several mantras rather consistently in our house over the years. Some are aimed at all of us: "We will watch our tones when speaking to each other." "We can be frustrated or even angry at each other, but we will learn to discuss our issues in a civil manner." Volume and cutting words are shut down pretty quickly in our home. Other of my rants are aimed at specific demographics, like my two boys. These are mainly prohibitions against various odors, fistfights, doors left open, and an uncanny forgetfulness on garbage day.

Others are meant for the female population in my home. A less-than-popular one heard from time to time: "I will not live in fear of female emotions." My point? I will not be manipulated either by tears or cold shoulders. This is not to suggest that the ladies in my house, or ladies in general, always resort to such juvenile tactics in order to get their way. (Did you notice that? I just violated the principle by qualifying my statement. After all, I would not want to incur the wrath of the female reader who took offense to such brazen misogyny.)

In truth, this motto is meant for me. The emphasis here is more about being a consistent leader. Too often leaders avoid making the right decision out of self-preservation or a desire to be popular. Honestly, I've done only so well with this one. My girls own me. I keep repeating the mantra despite my hypocrisy. It seems I walk around saying it to no avail. By now it's white noise, or a harmless bromide.

But finally getting to the point of this chapter, there is one additional proverb I've almost exclusively directed at my daughter: "We will not gain our self-worth from the fleeting affections of another human being." On this point I've been unrelenting. This one I am passionate about. I rather desperately want her to hear it. I've been restating it to her all her life. I cannot number the times I have reminded her. This one is more often directed to this sweet beauty residing under my care *because* she is particularly susceptible to violating it or being ruined by the very lie it's attempting to expose. "I know, Daddy," she assures me. "I won't," no doubt rolling the eyes of her heart as she says those words.

My intention is simple. I want my daughter to gain her self-image and self-worth as it arises primarily from biblical realities and not superficial unrealities set forth by our culture (or the fickle attention of teenage boys, otherwise known as my mortal enemy). I know she will succumb. For certain she has from time to time. How could she not? The culture has been carpet-bombing her feminine psyche with a vain self-focus and trendy insecurities since she was old enough to recognize her own face in a mirror.

I tell my daughter how beautiful she is rather often. There are those classic dad-and-daughter scenes during which she descends the stairs in formal attire headed to some school function or recital. I both love and hate that moment. I'm usually cleaning my shotguns in my mind. (Man, I despise teenage boys.) What comes out is filtered for her encouragement. "Wow! You are so beautiful." She needs to hear it from me.

Any father who remains silent at this moment is negligent and naïve. My own daughter thrives in my affection and attention. But my daughter also knows that my love for her is not contingent upon her physical beauty. I love who she is beneath all of that, which makes her adorable to me as her father. There is a true beauty there. This depth of love raises my daughter above vanity to personal security. She is adored.

My greatest concern for her is that she will give her heart to a man who does not see what I see.

We might assume the fear of man is a problem reserved for the male population. As it is, the discussion about man-fearing tendencies seems almost exclusively masculine in nature. No doubt it is a problem for men. But we would be greatly mistaken if we assumed it was an exclusively male problem.

The desire for approval is no respecter of gender. I would argue that on a certain level, it is more prominent among females than males. Honestly, are women any less concerned about perception and approval? Of course not. They are suffocated by it their entire lives. Being a woman can be treacherous. More treacherous than men imagine. It ain't easy being a girl. It's flat-out dangerous.

Think I'm exaggerating? Then obviously you've never witnessed the most vicious and ruthless predator on the planet. Not great white sharks or man-eating Sumatran tigers. Teenage girls. Teenage girls are to the female gender what ultimate fighting is to the competitive fighting world. To them, school is a virtual octagon. Junior high declares jihad on adolescent girls. A teenage girl in her prime makes Brock Lesnar—all six-feet-three and 287 pounds of him—seem like a softie. Teenage girls are the kraken of the adolescent world. Venomous and lethal. They frighten me. I've seen firsthand the carcasses they leave behind. My daughter has experienced moments of unbelievable betrayal by supposedly the best of friends. A loyal friend rejected all for the sake of gaining entry into the "in crowd." Popularity. Parties. Boys. Latest styles. The inner circle. Invitations to the dance. Whispers in the hallway. Rumors. Don't get in their way. They will destroy you. Run!

THE INNER "STAGE MOM"

Women are more inclined to need acceptance more often. For certain, they are more sensitive to when acceptance is missing. That "women are more emotional and sensitive" stuff is dead-on. If there is the slightest dip in my disposition due to weariness from work, or a lack of sleep, or a bad attitude, my daughter's radar is on high alert. First question: "Dad, is there something I've done?" I'm like, "What are you talking about?" "Well, you've been so quiet." It's like living with a therapist specializing in momentary depressive states.

But these are the contours of the female landscape. It is the environment in which they live and breathe. They are conditioned by the culture to care deeply for what people think about them. This is no less true for adult women. The perception—as a wife or mom—that you aren't living up to acceptable norms in appearance or standards of living can be devastating. This is especially true of ladies living in the shallow trenches of the American suburbs. Rare is the young lady or middle-aged mom who is free of the bondage of what others think.

Certain moms don't help matters. They seem to pass this suffocating pressure down to their own daughters. "No wire hangers!" The relative popularity of their daughters can become an all-consuming goal in their own life. Mothers and daughters seem to follow a similar pattern as that observed in fathers and sons. Moms too can live vicariously through their daughters. The only real difference is that dads are pressuring their sons from the sidelines of a sports field. Moms place the same pressure on their daughters pacing back and forth as their daughters stand in front of a mirror.

Every mom has a "stage mom" lurking inside of her. My own wife laments this tendency in her mom. When she was a teenager, her mom obsessed about her weight and eating habits. Counting every calorie on her behalf. "You'll get fat if you eat that," she would say. Of course, my wife barely weighed 100 pounds. She is still petite. (Major brownie points with that sentence.) But regardless, she still hears her mom's implicit criticism every time she puts a bite of food in her mouth. In the same way middle-aged men grow up wishing they had their dad's approval, many middle-aged women may spend all of their adult lives still trying to please their moms. There is such a thing as a "mommy wound."

Just to be clear, I'm not being prudish or puritanical. Asceticism is no less a virtue than vanity. Girls want to be considered attractive. Physical attraction and beauty are a valid part of it. I get it. But they are not all of it—as we have rather incessantly implied. Honestly, I did not go looking for the most "unattractive" person I could find. Not hardly. I was knocked off my feet by this blonde walking the halls of my high school with the bluest eyes I have ever seen. Although she turned me down flat the first few times I asked her out, I persisted. Eventually she gave up altogether and married me. Those same eyes still slay me today. Mutual attraction is part of God's design. God does not shy away from this in His Word. Have you read the Song of Solomon?

> How beautiful you are, my darling, how beautiful you are! Your eyes are like doves behind your veil; your hair is like a flock of goats that have descended from Mount Gilead. Your teeth are like a flock of newly shorn ewes which have come up from their washing, all of which bear twins, and not one among them has lost her young. Your lips are like a scarlet thread, and your mouth is lovely. Your temples are like a slice of a pomegranate behind your veil. Your neck is like the tower of David, built with rows of stones, on which are hung a thousand shields, all the round shields of the mighty men. Your two breasts are like two fawns, twins of a gazelle which feed among the lilies. Until the cool of the day when the shadows flee away, I will go my way to the mountain of myrrh and to the hill of frankincense. You are altogether beautiful, my darling, and there is no blemish in you (Song of Solomon 4:1-7 NASB).

Not sure why a woman would want her neck described as a "tower," but whatever. It was a long time ago. Regardless, the point is obvious. These two lovers were physically attracted to each other and expressing their attraction to one another was an important part of their relationship. After all, it is in writing. Being desired is not a bad thing, nor is making yourself attractive to your beloved. Romance is valid. As it is, young women are designed by God with a need to be desired and cherished.

It is the duty of the husband to reinforce his desire for his bride and, therefore, reinforce her beauty. For all the attention we have paid the Proverbs 31 woman, we seem to have missed the most obvious part.

It's a compliment. A tribute to a wife. Ultimately, it is a husband doting on his wife. Quite literally, it was a compliment of biblical proportions. An exhaustive list of why he loves and cherishes his wife. For all the applications we've made from this proverb for women and all the moralizing that has resulted, the husband's affection for his wife seems to be the most obvious one. Too often, husbands fail miserably in this area. We don't have a list. If we do, it's of complaints. Of course, we don't actually write them down. They slip out in comments here and there. But compliments go missing. And we wonder why middle-age women get tangled up in "emotional affairs" or track down old flames on social media. There is a reason Facebook is called the middle-age woman's porn.

There will come a time when our outward appearance fails us and cannot be depended on to secure the attention of others. Gravity wins. Time catches up. Lines mar our appearance. Beauty is fleeting. When we are young, appearance occupies such a substantial portion of our perspective. We judge each other based on the relative symmetry of our physical features or size. We love what is lovely. In this there is an implicit condition on our "love" and on our devotion to others. "If you continue to be attractive and pleasing to me, I will continue to love you."

This is the root of so many failures and heartaches in our society. It is the reason men walk away from wives and families. It is the reason young husbands have no sense of tenderness toward their wives. It is a bent in our nature. It is the very thing of which I have warned my daughter. It is the very thing I have attempted to protect my wife from by a consistent demonstration of my affection for her.

THE SHAME OF MY SHALLOW HEART

Beauty is so misunderstood by humanity. So relative in nature. So often missed by fickle human beings. So shallow. There is so much that is beautiful which is not seen. Not all beauty is aesthetic in nature, or perfectly symmetrical in nature. There is a type of beauty that is unseen. There is also a type of love that is blind. It cares most for the soul. It is attracted to the person. It transcends the superficial and is immune to the effects of time. It is not conditioned upon appearance or the sustainability of an ideal. It is least of all fickle. It is unconditional. It is this type of love that frees us from the bondage of the fear of man or the need to be accepted based on appearance or performance.

I recently watched a documentary about a nine-year-old boy suffering from Treacher Collins syndrome. My wife and children were all piled up in our bed watching it together. It was a profound moment for all of us. Treacher Collins is a genetic disorder that affects the structure of the face and results in a severe facial disfigurement. In certain cases, there is very little that resembles a normal human appearance.

The documentary chronicled the experience of this young man and his family as they faced the biases of a beauty-obsessed culture. This precious and innocent nine-year-old boy suffered from a prejudice that is hard to fathom. Enduring incessant stares in public. Being avoided on playgrounds. In some instances, having parents remove their children from his presence due to the "scary" effect of his appearance. It was another shameful display of humanity at its worst. Another occurrence of humanity missing the point of being human.

I was ashamed of myself. For I bear the marks of that same shallow intolerance for "different than me." We are a wicked bunch. What are we to make of ourselves when the most "civil" among us so easily and callously toss the soul of a precious human being aside due to an abnormality? Who is really deformed in all this?

At one point the documentary presents an interview with the boy's dad. He had witnessed firsthand the constant barrage of rejection his son had suffered over the years. He had long ago given up protesting the lack of consideration offered by the gawking eyes of his community. There was nothing that could be done. His objections had fallen on the deaf ears of a society blind to its prejudices. His anger toward others at the inequity had morphed into pity. His definitions of beauty and love had been transformed by what others considered unlovely. In tears, he confessed that his son—at the young age of nine—possessed a strength of person he would never have. His boy, so abhorrent to the norms of a petty people, loved those same people with an unconditional love they were all desperately looking for. How mysterious that a love for others is purified in one who is told he is undeserving of affection. How transcendent that a father watching his son consistently rejected by the culture learned what acceptance truly is.

At the end, the father turned to the camera and appealed to this vacancy in our perceptions: "I would encourage you, when you encounter someone with a facial disfigurement, to stop your natural tendencies. It's possible you might learn what true beauty is. My son's soul is the most beautiful thing I have ever seen." How rare is such perception.

This, then, is the very thing I have wanted my daughter to understand. Security and self-worth do not result from being acceptable or in becoming acceptable. They do not result from someone finding you lovely. True security and peace of heart result in finding acceptance when you are not acceptable, or in being loved when you are unlovely.

This is the fundamental mind-blowing reality in the gospel. A reality that runs contrary to all our misapprehension as human beings. You are accepted not because you are acceptable, but simply because God loves you. It has to be this way because we are all unlovely. He loved when you did not deserve His love. He poured His grace on you when you least deserved His affection. You are accepted not because of who you are, but simply because He loves you. You are loved not because of what you have done, but because of what He has done. Christianity turns all of our reality on its head. The gospel stands in perfect opposition to all of our nonsense. God loves what is unlovely.

SAFE
Julianna Zobrist

You know me
You know where I've been
You've felt the pain of my unfaithfulness
Your anger burned against me
But only for a time
Forgiveness has a way of saying "You are mine"

I will sing and I won't hide
You're the groom and I the blushing bride
I am safe with you
With you

You have hung a promise in the sky
A rainbow of colour to remind
That I am yours and you are mine
Yes I've been bought at a price

I will sing and I won't hide
You're the groom and I the blushing bride
I am safe with you
With you

I've broken every vow that I have sworn
I've placed upon your head a crown of thorns
You have no obligation any more
But still you choose
To call me yours

I will sing and I won't hide
You're the groom and I the blushing bride
I will sing and I won't hide
You're the groom and I the blushing bride
I am safe with you
With you

Used with permission.

The only time a woman really succeeds in changing a man is when he is a baby.

10

HUSBANDS—SERIOUSLY, YOU CANNOT CHANGE HIM

I was at an engagement party for a young couple in our church. There was a lot of hope and joy bound up in this intimate little celebration. For the most part, the guests meandered about picking at appetizers and downloading the latest adventures from each other's lives. At one stage we were ushered into the living room in order to personalize our well wishes for the couple. Scripture was read. We prayed over them. Our host then gave us an assignment. Each person from each couple present was to offer some advice to these young people heading toward matrimony.

They were to offer a principle hewn from their own experience that would aid the engaged couple in the beginning of theirs. It was supposed to be offered from a "I wish I knew now what I didn't know then" perspective. So we went around the room offering wisdom. The predictable litany of advice was offered. Pray together. Don't go to bed angry. You've heard it all before. It was a mixture of the benign and the inspiring. That is, until it got around to an elderly couple who was there.

They were in their early seventies and into the fifth decade of their marriage. The wife spoke first. She turned and looked at her husband for what seemed to be a prolonged period of time. As he was nearly deaf and had no idea what was happening, he was looking sleepily at the floor. The wife had a look of real sadness on her face. It was somewhere between pity and regret. She then turned back and looked right into the soul of the young wife and said, "Just remember, no matter how bad it gets for you, it could have been worse."

The brief dribble of laughter in the room was soon muffled by the awareness that she was serious. It was the cumulative effect of five decades of unhappiness seeping out onto the moment. The entire room went awkward. Sensing that his wife had said something, the elderly husband blurted out, "Heh? Did you say something?" It was a painful illustration of her life. Before she could answer him, I seized the sacerdotal moment and closed in prayer.

I can't think of a more depressing summary of 50 years spent in a marriage. I wonder how many wives have such despair on the tips of their tongues but lack the courage of five decades to say it. Retrospectively, I suppose it might have been the most important piece of inadvertent counsel the couple received that day. The elderly woman's rather pregnant expression contained a bit of hard realism. "Know what you are getting into. There is no going back."

FACING REALITY

Young women driven by the incessant ticking of biological clocks, or love, or lust, or fantasy, or numerous other unseen forces (which dads will never understand or accept) will determine to marry a man, and in so doing take upon themselves a fixer-upper. A man becomes a lifelong project of sorts. The marriage becomes a quest to create from the raw materials of a generally acceptable man the man of a young girl's dreams.

There is a shortsightedness at a certain stage in a young woman's life which, if it goes unchecked, will allow her to overlook obvious deficiencies in a man and proceed on toward marriage with a smile on her heart. All the while, as she approaches the union, she does so with an unbreakable hope in hope itself. She assumes he will change over time, or that she can change him by force. It's not as if she is totally unaware of who he really is. Indeed, to a degree she is aware. But it's the prospect of what he might become that blocks her view of the inevitable. He is who he is.

What she's attempting—to change a man's nature—has been tried countless times. And countless times, it has ended in the same place—failure. It cannot be done. And we should know this, but we try anyway. Months into the marriage, the reality sets in. Those traits that were winked at previously are now surprisingly acute. The manifestations of gentleness and consideration that were present in limited supply at the start are all but absent now.

Eventually you get down to the real man. Counsel is sought from a trusted friend or pastor. This ends in an awkward moment of awareness. It's usually a rather implicit and painful "I told you so." Calls are made to mom in attempts to unburden her conscience. But this only makes matters worse, given that mom finds herself in a very similar predicament. The young wife ends up living in a strange land of commiseration among frustrated wives. She ventures wearily along, wondering if she made a huge mistake. It feels like a bait-and-switch took place. But, it was her own heart that created the illusion.

PAIN IN THE BOOTH NEXT TO ME

It's not uncommon for me to be in a coffee shop somewhere writing and have a pair of wives sit nearby. Crammed in among each other perched at these little tables, you can't help but hear other people's conversations. I don't mean to eavesdrop, but I inadvertently pick up tidbits. (I usually go for the Bose noise-cancelling headphones.) Sometimes (very often, in fact) the talk turns to the marriage and the relative participation of the husband. "He doesn't understand this..." "He does not seem to care about that..." "I tried to talk to him about this..." The normal kind of stuff. Usually, one friend does all the talking and the other all the listening. The talker speaks in whispery tones like some secret agent. The friend simply listens—sometimes for an hour or more—interjecting occasionally with some sensitive-sounding question. "Really?" "Are you serious?" Once the talker gets it all out, they hug and depart. Nothing is resolved.

My guess? If we went back in time and could be flies on the wall at the start of a relationship, we'd hear the same descriptions of the man coming from a concerned friend or counselor. The young woman no doubt knew these things about him, but chose not to listen. With the potential of marriage looming in the balance, it's easy to ignore the warning signs.

Those small patterns in a man's life that we easily dismiss as minor (or manageable) early on in the relationship tend to carry the greatest weight in the long run. An inability (or unwillingness) to communicate his feelings or deal with issues leads to mounds of unresolved conflict later in life. A lack of discipline with finances creates serious tension and discontent. The absence of life goals and a prospective future leave her serving as a life coach for the husband. A view toward sex that is more akin to that of an adolescent than someone on the brink of marriage later manifests itself in deep resentment and pain. An immature response to conflict that results in a tendency to escape, a sharp defensiveness, or a brooding poutiness eventually develops into an angry silence. A preoccupation with trivial things (video games, recreation, sports) becomes an escape route leading away from the elephant in the marriage.

It's not that a man must be perfect before he qualifies for marriage. That's unrealistic, and unfair to boot. Women would be no less disqualified under such restraints. There would be no marriages ever if perfection were the standard. Nor is it proper to set idealistic conditions upon a man—"You need to be this way in this area before I can marry you." This is narcissistic. Furthermore, it never works anyway. Besides, he will do whatever you tell him to do for as long as necessary in order to marry you. Disappointment is inevitable when we put our faith in the relative quality of another human being, or in the hopes that the person may one day make us happy.

THE HOUSEWIFE'S PORN

Much has been made about pornography among men and rightfully so. There is currently an epidemic moral failure underway among husbands. This includes Christian husbands. I've dealt with it pretty regularly as a pastor. Its effects are devastating and long-lasting. Often the root of the struggle can be traced back to unrealistic or primarily secular views of sexuality and imbalanced expectations of the wife in the marriage bed. When disappointment sets in, men can drift toward some adolescent fantasy readily available online. The discovery of files on a husband's computer by a completely unsuspecting wife is an all-too-common occurrence.

But there is a similar drift that can occur in the wife's life. It too is rooted in same type of disappointment within a marriage. It's the same type of force that may lead a husband toward pornography, or actual adultery. Unlike the husband's sin, it's not a physical temptation, but an emotional one. Disappointed with the emotional commitment of the husband, or how he turned out within the marriage, she goes searching for a memory and a foregone dream of marital bliss.

This is where social media can serve as a sort of emotional pornography, luring a discontented wife's heart away from the bond of marriage. It happens in the same manner that a husband searches out pornographic images. Facebook becomes a sort of porn for the unhappy housewife. I've seen it all too often. A wife locates a high school flame, makes contact, and an emotional affair is under way. Not much unlike when a husband confesses his struggle with porn, her admission of an emotional bond with another man can have a permanent effect on the marriage. Trust breaks down. Deep anger sets in.

Too often the roots of this type of betrayal are laid down years before in the beginning of the relationship. Specifically, it's that pesky hope that one can create the man of one's dreams from the man you actually end up marrying. As time passes and reality sets in, wives grow resentful of their circumstances. A lack of respect toward the husband settles in. Intimacy becomes an infrequent and cold obligation. It's a recipe for disaster. Eventually, the name of a high school flame is entered in a search window. Before long, the husband is calling me asking me what he should do. He never saw it coming.

What We Can't Change Grace Accepts

When I say you cannot change him, I don't necessarily mean you should not marry him. I mean you should accept who he is as a person before you do. Fact is, we go in blind. We've no real understanding of the other person's character. We're clueless about where they consistently struggle as people, or the places in them that need the most growth.

We do more research when buying a car than when getting to know our future mate. Rather than going into relationships ready to identify weaknesses, we go in pretending they don't exist. But we should face them head on. This awareness does not diminish the love we have for the other person, but pushes it deeper. You need to be able to pinpoint the aspects of his life that will make him hard to live with or follow as God's appointed leader of your life. Before you determine to commit your life to him, you need to know who he is truly.

The point is to face the tendencies of his life head on in the beginning and ask yourself if you can serve this person. Frankly, he should do the same with you. There should be an openness and transparency about who you two are. The good and the bad. Otherwise you'll have no real sense of who the other person really is.

Too often the changes we seek to effect in our husband are not the ones God has in mind anyway. They're the changes we want. The ones that would make us happier. We're merely serving ourselves by forcing our preferences upon his life. Or we're constantly comparing him to dear old dad, or some fantasy. But that man you fell in love with is not going to change in any great measure over the duration of his life. I know this sounds bleak, but it's what you need to hear.

Of course, this is not to say he won't grow spiritually or mature personally. God does change people. But it is to say he will not up end up becoming the man of your dreams if he was nowhere near it to begin with. That just doesn't happen. If this does happen, it's usually because grace allowed us to love the man God gave us and not because we woke up one day lying next to Fabio.

If your guy is more the quiet type, he will always be that way. If he has no clue which side of the plate the fork goes on, he may frequently embarrass you at formal occasions. If he is not handy with tools, you can expect everything he touches around the house to be almost fixed. If he's tight with money, don't be surprised if he recycles coffee grounds.

If he wears plaid on every date, expect black socks and sandals on the beach. It's who he is. And who he is has been informed by years of training and tradition. It no doubt runs in his family.

Paul Tripp has mentioned that we approach marriage the same way a person goes about selling a used car. We polish up the exterior. Vacuum the debris of life from off the floorboards. Touch up the blemishes. When someone shows interest, we distract their attention from what's wrong by pointing out what's right. We want them to see only the acceptable things.

Tripp was spot-on here. We sell ourselves to each other by emphasizing our more favorable features. It's only after we've driven around in a car for a while that we begin to notice all the imperfections. Squeaks. Rattles. Malfunctioning electronics. Sticking doors. Rust on the bumper. Stains on the carpet.

When it comes to marriage—especially under the Christian construct—we need to know about the dings and dents. We, more than most, should know they are there. "All have sinned and fall short of the glory of God" makes this clear.

And grace equips us to love a person despite their shortcomings. In Christ, we've been loved the same way.

APPLICATION FOR PERMISSION
TO DATE MY DAUGHTER

NOTE: This application will be incomplete and rejected unless accompanied by a complete financial statement, job history, lineage, and current medical report from your doctor.

Name_____ Date of birth_____

Height_____ Weight_____ IQ_____ GPA_____

Social Security #_____ Driver's license #_____

Boy Scout rank and badges _____

Home address _____

City/State _____ Zip_____

Do you have parents? ___Yes ___No

Is one male and the other female? ___Yes ___No

If no, explain: _____

_____

_____

Number of years they have been married _____

If less than your age, explain: _____

_____

_____

Accessories Section:

A. Do you own or have access to a van? __Yes __No

B. A truck with oversized tires? __Yes __No

C. A waterbed? __Yes __No

D. A pickup with a mattress in the back? __Yes __No

E. A tattoo? __Yes __No

F. Do you have an earring, nose ring, pierced tongue, pierced cheek, or a belly button ring? __Yes __No

(If you answered yes to any of the above, discontinue filling out the application and leave the premises immediately. I suggest running.)

Essay Section:

In 50 words or less, what does *late* mean to you?

_____
_____
_____

In 50 words or less, what does *don't touch my daughter* mean to you?

_____
_____
_____

In 50 words or less, what does *abstinence* mean to you?

_____
_____
_____

References Section:

Church you attend _____

How often you attend _____

When would be the best time to interview your

     Father? _____

     Mother? _____

     Pastor? _____

Short-Answer Section:
Answer by filling in the blank. Please answer freely; all answers are confidential.

A. If I were shot, the last place I would want to be shot would be:

_____

B. If I were beaten, the last bone I would want broken is my:

_____

C. A woman's place is in the:

_____

D. The one thing I hope this application does not ask me about is:

_____

E. What do you want to do IF you grow up?_____

_____

_____

F. When I meet a girl, the thing I always notice about her first is:

_____

G. What is the current going rate of a hotel room?

_____

I swear that all information supplied above is true and correct to the best of my knowledge under penalty of death, dismemberment, Native American ant torture, crucifixion, electrocution, Chinese water torture, and red-hot pokers.

_____

Applicant's signature (that means sign your name, moron!)

_____

Mother's signature   Father's signature

_____

Pastor/Priest/Rabbi/State Representative/Congressman

Thank you for your interest, and it had better be genuine and nonsexual.

Please allow four to six years for processing.

You will be contacted in writing if you are approved. Please do not try to call or write (since you probably can't, and it would cause you injury). If your application is rejected, you will be notified by two gentlemen wearing white ties and carrying violin cases. (You might watch your back.)

A brief explanation of this chapter: Over the years of ministry, I've had the catbird seat on God's grace in people's lives. I've watched Him work in impossible situations. His power to work in the lives of His people has been breathtaking. I've seen those who have suffered great pain worship. Those full of intense anger forgive. Those hardened break. The irreconcilable reconciled. I've also seen the completely powerless exert more force of faith than any of those in positions of power and influence. In Christ's economy, everything is upside down. Great is small. Weak is strong. Broken is healed. Most all the time life is not like we think or prefer. God works in mysterious ways. The most mysterious has always been when broken and sinful people choose to live upside down. This chapter is dedicated to a Christian woman, wife, and mom who proved God's power and gave me another view of His grace. I use her letter by permission.

II

STRENGTH—YOU *CANNOT* DO ALL THINGS IN CHRIST

Y ou can't actually "do all things" in Christ. Not the way you think you can. I realize this sounds like sacrilege given the suburban spin we've put on this biblical expression, but it's true. Paul did not intend some sort of personal triumphalism here. He couldn't "do all things" either. He could not get out of prison—which is where he penned this verse—no matter how intensely he believed in Jesus. He was stuck there until God determined otherwise. But he could "be imprisoned" in Christ, who strengthened him to be imprisoned. Prison is such a good place to discover Christ's sufficiency.

The true meaning of "all things" might disappoint contemporary Christians. But it shouldn't. The actual point is even more glorious than the suburban legend. It gets us so much closer to grace. We normally take it to mean something like "I can do anything I set my mind to if I simply believe." That is, I can achieve any personal goal by faith. Get this job. Win this game. Ace this test. But the verse has little (or nothing) to do with our personal achievement in the face of severe odds.

It's not about our achievements at all. It's about Christ's achievement and a constant dependence on Him regardless of one's station in life—good or bad. Besides, there's a real danger in applying it the way we're prone to. What if you can't "do" it? What if things don't work out—no matter how much you believe? Your failure might call into question the goodness of God, or the sufficiency of Christ. It robs countless hurting and weak people of the truth here. There is power in weakness.

A more accurate translation of the principle is "I can trust in Christ (and the benefits of His life, death, and resurrection) even when I can't achieve a personal goal. I can fail to achieve my goals and still trust my Savior's love. Or, I can have cancer. Or, I can lose everything. Or, I can be fired. I can 'do all this' because of who Jesus is." It's the unpredictable swings of life (want and prosperity) that Paul was able to traverse by focusing on the work of Christ. This is the "all things" he has in view here. For Paul, Jesus' righteous life made seasons of poverty seem like wealth and seasons of wealth seem like poverty. He could experience all these things without falling into despair on one side or idolatry on the other.

Point is, Christ is sufficient even when I can't change things. Or when my circumstance has the potential to change me. I can be in the worst place of my entire life with joy and peace because Christ is infinitely better. So when I can't change my state of affairs, the person of Christ sustains me. What Paul is saying goes way beyond the point of our usual rendering. "If I'm in a circumstance where there is nothing I can do, I can still do that in Christ." I can do nothing, if need be, and keep Christ as the supreme object of my faith. The things we are able to do are much greater than personal goals. They are the things of life.

I've seen the truth of this verse lived out by people in the midst of life's worst hardships. I've witnessed this truth come to *life* when people were near *death*. I have seen people who could *do nothing* actually *do all things*. Recently, a beloved young mom in our church who was being divorced by her unbelieving husband put the power of this verse on display for me. One Sunday morning, per her request, she stood (festooned with the full support of her elders) before the church family as she explained her husband's absence, sought the prayers of the body, and exalted the sufficiency of Christ.

The church rallied with unbelievable grace and compassion to her situation. Her faith was remarkable. It was hard to believe that she could be so poised in such a dark moment. But this is Paul's point. She was able to "be divorced" in Christ who strengthened her. She could do even this. Afterward, this is the letter she wrote to her leadership expressing her faith in Christ and her love for Him. I use it with permission.

Sunday Afternoon
Byron and Elders,

When I started to write this letter a week ago, it was a letter I was going to write to friends and family about what was going on in my marriage. I was writing about all the details of what's been going on this past year. (Probably too much detail.) I basically was writing a sob story of "look at me, look at my pain, and look at what my husband did to me."

How wrong I was. So very wrong to even write such words. Very unloving…and if I might…very un-Christlike. Today (Sunday) I was lovingly reminded, encouraged, and humbled that I am part of a body of believers. I am to use my gifts, my life, my TRIALS and my JOY (in my trials) to encourage the body to look to the Lord and not me. I have had times this past year that I have felt that my suffering was not fair. Or I have felt that I have had good reason for the way I was reacting to my trial (when self-pity would set in). Well, today I saw a body of believers who did not know all the details encourage another part of the body in a life-altering trial. I didn't know how to ask for help, or know how to allow someone else's gift encourage me and redirect me to the Lord and see the Father, Son, and the Holy Spirit all get the credit and all work in unity!

The letter I first wrote has been deleted. And now a new one is being written thanking GOD for my trial. Thanking GOD for my suffering and for the ENDLESS amount of joy GOD has shown me in and through this. I know GOD was pleased today by our actions. Our church body's eyes were looking "up" at the Savior and not looking "at" the situation. While I stood there, I actually "forgot" all the ins and outs that brought me to that place of standing there. I sensed an endless amount of peace from God through the work of the Spirit, and He calmed my anxious heart.

I don't know how the Spirit was moving today in everyone else, and what He was doing in their hearts. I can just tell you that the SPIRIT was at work in my life to teach me to love others. Love the lost (for I too was once a slave to sin), love the body of Christ (they have all been given gifts to be used to glorify GOD, not me), and ultimately love the Lord with all I am (while I was a sinner…and I still am, Christ died for me).

My prayer is now as David prayed in Psalm 27, and beautifully written by Nancy Leigh DeMoss:

> "Lord Jesus, You have shown me that only one thing is absolutely necessary, and that is the one thing I want to seek after with all my heart: that I may live in Your presence every day of my life, that I may gaze upon Your beauty with a heart of worship and adoration, and that I may learn to know Your heart, Your ways, and Your will. To this supreme purpose I dedicate myself. By Your grace, I will make this the highest daily priority of my life. Amen."

I am honored and humbled to be a part of this body, this church, and under the faithful "insanity" (I mean that as a compliment) teaching of a humbled servant of our Lord. Thank you for standing with me today, all of you.

May God ALONE get the glory and I be filled with HIS JOY.

Rule One:

If you pull into my driveway and honk you'd better be delivering a package, because you're sure not picking anything up.

Rule Two:

You do not touch my daughter in front of me. You may glance at her, so long as you do not peer at anything below her neck. If you cannot keep your eyes or hands off of my daughter's body, I will remove them.

Rule Three:

I am aware that it is considered fashionable for boys of your age to wear their trousers so loosely that they appear to be falling off their hips. Please don't take this as an insult, but you and all of your friends are complete idiots. Still, I want to be fair and open-minded about this issue, so I propose this compromise: You may come to the door with your underwear showing and your pants ten sizes too big, and I will not object. However, in order to ensure that your clothes do not, in fact, come off during the course of your date with my daughter, I will take my electric nail gun and fasten your trousers securely in place to your waist.

Rule Four:

I'm sure you've been told that in today's world, sex without utilizing a "barrier method" of some kind can kill you. Let me elaborate: When it comes to sex, I am the barrier, and I will kill you.

Rule Five:

It is usually understood that in order for us to get to know each other, we should talk about sports, politics, and other issues of the day. Please do not do this. The only information I require from you is an indication of when you expect to have my daughter safely back at my house, and the only word I need from you on this subject is *early*.

Rule Six:

I have no doubt you are a popular fellow, with many opportunities to date other girls. This is fine with me as long as it is okay with my daughter. Otherwise, once you have gone out with my little girl, you will continue to date no one but her until she is finished with you. If you make her cry, I will make you cry.

Rule Seven:

As you stand in my front hallway, waiting for my daughter to appear, and more than an hour goes by, do not sigh and fidget. If you want to be on time for the movie, you should not be dating. My daughter is putting on her makeup, a process that can take longer than painting the Golden Gate Bridge. Instead of just standing there, why don't you do something useful, like changing the oil in my car?

Rule Eight:

The following places are not appropriate for a date with my daughter: Places where there are beds, sofas, or anything softer than a wooden stool. Places where there is darkness. Places where there is dancing, holding hands, or happiness. Places where the ambient temperature is warm enough to induce my daughter to wear shorts, tank tops, midriff T-shirts, or anything other than overalls, a sweater, and a goose down parka—zipped up to her throat. Movies with strong romantic or sexual themes are to be avoided; movies which feature chain saws are okay. Hockey games are okay. Old folks' homes are better.

Rule Nine:

Do not lie to me. I may appear to be a potbellied, balding, middle-aged, dim-witted has-been. But on issues relating to my daughter, I am the all-knowing, merciless god of your universe. If I ask you where you are going and with whom, you have one chance to tell me the truth, the whole truth, and nothing but the truth. I have a shotgun, a shovel, and five acres behind the house. Do not trifle with me.

Rule Ten:

Be afraid. Be very afraid. It takes very little for me to mistake the sound of your car in the driveway for a chopper coming in over a rice paddy near Hanoi. When my Agent Orange starts acting up, the voices in my head frequently tell me to clean the guns as I wait for you to bring my daughter home. As soon as you pull into the driveway, you should exit the car with both hands in plain sight. Speak the perimeter password, announce in a clear voice that you have brought my daughter home safely and early, then return to your car—there is no need for you to come inside. The camouflaged face at the window is mine.

"I will put enmity between you and the woman, and between your offspring and her offspring; he shall bruise your head, and you shall bruise his heel." To the woman he said, "I will surely multiply your pain in childbearing; in pain you shall bring forth children. Your desire shall be for your husband, and he shall rule over you."

GENESIS 3:15-16

By grace you have been saved through faith. And this is not your own doing; it is the gift of God, not a result of works, so that no one may boast. For we are his workmanship, created in Christ Jesus for good works, which God prepared beforehand, that we should walk in them.

EPHESIANS 2:8-10

GRACE—
YOU MUST LOVE CHRIST MORE
TO LOVE HIM AS YOU SHOULD

The diatribe against men and masculinity is relentless and everywhere. Male bashing is a national pastime. Mocking the male species is the air breathed within popular culture. You can't escape it. Basically, men are idiots. Neanderthal-like creatures. Taylor Swift has sold the same song millions of times. (God have mercy on the future Mr. Taylor Swift.) Men are the punch line that accompanies the constant joke offered by everything from advertisements to situation comedies. It's one perpetual eye roll aimed at the idiocy of men.

I'd venture to say that without this thread, most advertising would all but disappear. We'd never sell anything. More than half of all popular forms of entertainment (television programs, movies, novels, music) would cease to exist. Seriously, if the depiction of men as completely incompetent people were to go away, Adele would have nothing to sing about. And try to imagine life without Adele. Such horror is hard to comprehend.

Generally, men are the foil against which women stand as the superior gender. Men are savage, dense, and generally handicapped by a lack of intelligence. Women are graceful, bright, and impeccably rational creatures. Men grunt, scratch, and eat their way through a given week. Women, on the other hand, grace the planet with tenderness, organization, and efficiency. Men think with their groins. (Of course this tendency goes without saying. Put a scantily clad, well-endowed woman next to a bag of fish heads, and men will buy it.) Women, on the other hand, think with their heads. Men lack any real capacity for emotion (except when angling for sex). Women, by contrast, are innately emotional creatures. Men cannot be trusted with infants, or be expected to keep track of their own children for more than an hour at a time. Women, by contrast, can be trusted to safely store weapons-grade uranium in their pantry next to the mac-n-cheese. The underlying message in all this is undeniable: Men are stupid. If men were more like women, the planet would be a better place.

WHEN EVIL MEN WANT STUFF

Not long ago something occurred to me. It's bothered me ever since. A lot of movies follow the same worn-out plot. It's almost always there. For the life of me, I can't think of a popular movie in the last ten years that hasn't followed it. (Outside of the romantic comedy genre, which I have no direct knowledge of.) The plot that I have in mind is infused with the aforementioned universal disdain for the male species. Almost every time I sit down in a theater, or rent a movie at home, it's there. At this stage it taunts me. I can't not see it. Even my beloved Bourne trilogy runs along this same redundant pathway. Nonetheless, I hold my nose and continue to watch it. As a writer, this absence of originality drives me crazy.

The plot goes something like this. Powerful, wealthy, and greedy men with an insatiable desire for more wealth and power destroy everything in their path to get what they want. (Some call this capitalism.) Underlying all the action and drama in the film is some greedy middle-aged man (often from another planet, or a strangely sadistic super villain) who did something unthinkably evil to get what he wanted. Trust me. The storyline is all over the place. Originality is scarce. Men are behind all the wickedness in the world.

Nothing is sacred. No measure of force is off limits. They will throw a sack full of puppies against a wall if it stands between them and their desired object. Destroy villages in third world countries to gain access to diamonds. Pour radioactive material from factories into alpine streams. Melt ice caps with laser beams to get at the oil underneath. Cut down centuries-old trees to build condos. They'll even rip the heads off stuffed animals if that's what it takes. Eventually a group of kids, a flying dog, or the local PTA with a female president rises up and defeats the evil of male greed. At the core of most scripts is the "men want stuff and destroy stuff to get it" mantra. Basic message? Men are the ubiquitous antagonists of humanity and the cause of all the evil that has ever occurred.

IT'S IN OUR HEADS

Regardless of how easily dismissible many of the more ridiculous portrayals may be, the general theme—men are idiots—is firmly implanted in the psyche of our culture, especially that of females. Who can resist the urge to roll the eyes when men obsess over obscure baseball statistics, paint their face on game day, come to the table with grease under their finger nails, or wear stripes with plaid? Morons. Right?

Whether consciously or unconsciously, this worn-out male stereotype is accepted as true. It's inevitable when one message washes out any other potential perception of men. Women are groomed to equate masculinity in its various forms (aggression, ruggedness, competition, etc.) with immaturity and adolescence. It would seem that masculinity is something to be overcome. Collectively, there seems to be an agreement that men need to grow out of masculinity.

Obviously, I don't agree. I reject the notion that behaviors basic to masculinity automatically signal irresponsibility or immaturity. In the very same way I don't assume the behaviors basic to natural femininity (emotion, sensitivity, delicateness) signal shallowness or weakness. Masculinity and maturity are not at odds. Nor are femininity and strength.

I actively encourage masculinity in my two sons. Guns, knives, insects, bloody noses, scrapes, spontaneous moments of risk, and the occasional brawl are all part of the experience. I've no fear that any of this will stunt their personal development. At the very same time, virtues essential to their character are being encouraged (self-awareness, spirituality, intelligence, self-discipline, responsibility, compassion). When these traits are wed with their masculinity, it will create a more effective servant leader and well-rounded person. For the record, I approach my daughter in a similar fashion. Because she is a female I don't assume she's incapable of certain things. I encourage capacities in my teenage daughter (self-confidence, leadership, hard work, determination) that will give her an advantage in her future as well.

Admittedly, in each case (men and women) certain stereotypes prove true. After all, stereotypes exist for a reason. There are men who seem to check every box on the "idiot list." But this phenomenon is not exclusive to the male species. I've encountered as many women who make Cruella De Vil seem like Mother Teresa. I've been in the ministry a long time. I've counseled thousands of couples. The notion that husbands are automatically to blame for the problems in a marriage is long gone. I've called as many wives back from the brink of disaster as I have men. I've seen as many wives ask their husband's forgiveness for sins committed against the marriage as I have men. Believe me. No one gender has the market cornered on stupidity.

IT'S ALWAYS THERE BENEATH THE PAIN

The most miserable marriages I've counseled over the years have had two consistent characteristics: neglect and disrespect. They're always there. A husband who lacks the tenderness necessary to care for his wife. A wife who can't bring herself to respect her husband. The husband ignores the wife's needs and spends the majority of his marriage abdicating his leadership. The wife thinks the husband is basically incompetent and has spent the entirety of the marriage driving this central point home. Regardless of the chaos on the surface, it most always stems from these twin realities between the surface. It creates a vicious sort of cycle in a marriage. Husband and wife feed off their disdain for the other.

It's not always possible to determine which came first—the neglect or the disrespect—but the origin of each is clear: the fall of mankind. The Bible predicted this mess when sin entered the world. The Word of God makes clear that the collateral damage of our rebellion would include the unique harmony of the husband and wife that originally existed in Eden.

> "I will put enmity between you and the woman, and between your offspring and her offspring; he shall bruise your head, and you shall bruise his heel." To the woman he said, "I will surely multiply your pain in childbearing; in pain you shall bring forth children. Your desire shall be for your husband, and he shall rule over you" (Genesis 3:15-16).

Well...that pretty much nails it. We're screwed up. Rather than self-sacrificing servitude, the husband tends toward a harsh sort of rule. Rather than a humble submission to the leadership of the husband, the wife seeks to overthrow his authority and take it upon herself.

This battle of the sexes has been playing itself out in one way or the other in every marriage since the beginning of time. Clearly, all of these struggles on each side are distortions of God's original design for marriage. Once there was a harmony, a beautiful unity in the diversity. One emerged out of two. No tyranny. No rebellion. No battle. Peace.

> Then the man said, "This at last is bone of my bones and flesh of my flesh; she shall be called Woman, because she was taken out of Man." Therefore a man shall leave his father and his mother and hold fast to his wife, and they shall become one flesh. And the man and his wife were both naked and were not ashamed (Genesis 2:23-25).

NOT ALL MEN ARE IDIOTS

I want to go on record: *Not all men fit the stereotype.* Not all men cop a feel every time a woman walks by. Not all men think of sex every 30 seconds. Not all men are incapable of sympathy. Not all men are unable to read the emotions of their wives. (Although it is still true that no husband can read his wife's mind.) Not all men neglect the call to spiritual leadership. Not all men are incompetent. Not all men are despotic. Not all men have given up on guiding their children. Not all men are married to their jobs. Not all men run off with another woman the moment their wife of 20 years begins to show her age. There are godly men out there. For certain, they're imperfect. But, they're Spirit-filled. They love Christ. There are virtuous, respectful, and capable men out there. I've seen them.

I also want to go on record with a related fact: *Men and women are different.* Venus and Mars different. Up and down different. His and hers different. We think differently. Feel differently. Need differently. Respond differently. Worry differently. We were created differently. Revolutionary, I know, but this fact seems to be ignored and almost constantly. Point: These differences are a really good thing. We need them to exist as a species.

So here's the question: Should the differences in one gender be viewed as inadequacies by the other? Or should they be celebrated? This is where most all of us have bought into the stereotypes. Too often we diminish the contribution of our spouses by viewing the distinguishing features of our genders as flaws. News flash: The world would not be a better place if men were more like women. Hello? There would be no world.

Let's think through this. Does competitiveness or aggression in a man automatically mean he is juvenile and lacks self-control? Should we roll our eyes and consider it immature when two grown men go after each other in a pickup basketball game? Does it mean they're dim and unthinking? Or how about when a husband desires sex more often than his wife? Our culture loves to pick on this trait. No doubt it's true, but should men be ashamed of it? Does this really mean sex is all men think about? Or that a husband is not interested in his wife on a personal level? Or that it's strictly physical for him without any emotional connection? If we consider how men and women are hard-wired from creation, I'd say this tendency is spot on. After all, aren't men supposed to be the pursuer? Furthermore, don't wives have a need to be considered desirable by their husbands? Or am I just grasping at straws here?

We always seem to be attempting to pull one gender toward the traits of the other. Wives need to think and act like their husbands.

Husbands need to think and act like their wives. In so doing we are working against the complimentary relationship ordained by the Creator. The distinctions fit together in the most unique relationship on the planet. The unity from our diversity can be observed at every level. Even in our physiology reveals the unique symmetry formed out of our distinct makeups: "Therefore a man shall leave his father and mother and hold fast to his wife, and the two shall become one flesh" (Ephesians 5:31).

This is not to deny the other side of this discussion. Our genders are also very similar. As created beings, men and women have many qualities in common. Characteristics innate to humanity. As spiritual beings, we were each created bearing the image of God. But accompanying those similarities are very distinct differences. Yet they are not opposed to each other. They fit each other. And those differences (emotional, physical, mental, intuitive) join together in marriage to bring glory to God as the two become one and display the dominion of God upon the earth. That now-famous line "you complete me" is rather cheesy, but it has a lot of truth to it. Men and women do complete each other. Maguire was on to something.

The stereotype is hard to get away from. It's universal. Christian marriages are no exception. Once this way of thinking trickles down into the marriage, Christian or not, it's hard to root out. Many women enter into marriage with it downloaded into their mind-set. It may be subtle, but it's usually there. It may be innocent, but it has an effect. An eye roll here. An exasperated sigh there. A complaint offered about the husband to a group of friends. The general sense that the wife places no real confidence in her husband's ability.

THE SELF-FULFILLING PROPHECY
OF A MALE STEREOTYPE

Over time it accumulates. It erodes the concept of unity within the marriage. It destroys the idea of partnership. It diminishes the contribution of an equal partner. It depletes the husband's confidence. Believe me, he feels it. He knows it's there. A husband feels the disrespect of his wife more than he feels anything else. After years of being told he's incompetent (whether explicitly, or implicitly), he's happy to play along. It's like a self-fulfilling prophecy.

I've seen this so many times. It's very predictable. I know this man. He's hard to miss. Lifeless. Defeated. I hurt for him. So many husbands are in bondage to the pervasive male stereotype. It's been driven home by the wife over years of disrespect and low expectations. It's usually never overt. But it is relentless. It's a well-disguised snide comment. It's a very subtle but public display of disrespect. It's an embarrassed apology for the husband's inability to communicate his feelings offered at dinner conversation. It's an obvious distrust in the husband's leadership. It's a hundred predicable clichés: "There are three children in my home—my two kids and my husband."

Over time, little pieces of contempt pile up and crush a man's spirit. What you're left with is tragic. Emasculation. You may learn to ignore the barrage of disrespect reigning down from the culture, but it's hard to ignore when it sleeps beside you at night.

Holding these stereotypes over each other and diminishing the contribution of our spouse is such a graceless way to live. Are we really so shallow after having beheld grace to treat each other this way? Viewing a husband as a buffoon who can't tie his shoes without the aid of his wife denies the grace of God. Viewing a wife as a domineering control freak who uses passive aggression to get her way ignores the cross.

It is possible to diminish my spouse only by exalting myself. It is possible to exalt myself only by ignoring my own depravity and failure. It is possible to ignore my own depravity and failure only by ignoring the sacrifice of Christ. Neither the husband nor wife is anywhere close to perfection. No contribution better than the other. There is no place within a Christian marriage for such arrogance. All healthy marriages are populated by two people who assume their sin is the real issue with the marriage.

Let me be clear: I'm not whining about all this. I've got a thick skin. I can handle the derision. It's where I live. But if Christian couples are going to operate on this level—even in slightest degrees—they'll have to face some serious contradictions. For example, this attitude denies the power of God to change a person. Ultimately, these worn-out stereotypes leave no room for the hope of the gospel. It's such a graceless frame of reference.

Can God not change a man? Can a man be transformed by the grace of God? Are there not men out there who—by the grace of God—are beating the odds? We live within view of Calvary. The cross gets us past these hateful generalizations. It liberates us from selfish and critical tendencies that take us captive. Calvary speaks to us before it speaks to anyone else. In so doing it drags us back to the harmony of Eden. It makes us grateful for the companionship found only in the bonds of marriage. It creates a spirit of servitude. It empowers us to overlook the imperfections in another person and be grateful for the forgiveness of God toward our own lives.

So your husband is imperfect. So your husband did not turn out as you anticipated. So your husband does not do things the way you prefer. Or in the time you prefer. So your husband has failed you a time or two. So your husband has flaws. Of course he does. But is the respect for him—to which you have been called by Christ—dependent upon anything in him? Can you love and respect him despite the presence of such inadequacies? Yes. But only in the cross. Reciprocally, is his service of you dependent upon your respect of him? Of course not. Otherwise he would never have due cause to serve you.

We are right down to the essence of grace. If Christ's love toward us was contingent upon any quality or action in us we would never know his love. But Christ's love is unconditional. It was not conditioned upon anything in man because sinful man could not meet any condition. It was all of grace. Jesus met the condition of righteousness. Is it any wonder that Christian marriage is rooted in the mystery of the cross?

> Wives, submit to your own husbands, as to the Lord. For the husband is the head of the wife even as Christ is the head of the church, his body, and is himself its Savior. Now as the church submits to Christ, so also wives should submit in everything to their husbands. Husbands, love your

wives, as Christ loved the church and gave himself up for her, that he might sanctify her, having cleansed her by the washing of water with the word, so that he might present the church to himself in splendor, without spot or wrinkle or any such thing, that she might be holy and without blemish (Ephesians 5:22-27).

Is it any wonder that any specific instruction on marriage was preceded by a description of saving grace?

By grace you have been saved through faith. And this is not your own doing; it is the gift of God, not a result of works, so that no one may boast. For we are his workmanship, created in Christ Jesus for good works, which God prepared beforehand, that we should walk in them (Ephesians 2:8-10).

RESPECT—ROCKET FUEL FOR THE MALE SOUL

There's nothing strikes a chord in a husband's soul like the respect of his wife. It taps into the primitive harmony of God's design for husband and wife echoing back from Eden. Does the gospel call for such respect? Yes. Does a husband really deserve it? No. He's a sinner. Which is why heartfelt respect is so hard.

Respect is no easy task. But great duties are usually fulfilled in light of superior incentives. You have an immense duty as a wife. You are called of God to follow an imperfect leader. To respect another broken human being. To entrust yourself to a fallen creature complete with imperfections. I am a husband. So I get what you are up against.

Ultimately, there has to be something superior to your husband for you to live toward your husband as you should. If you condition your role within marriage on your husband, you are destined for frustration. There has to be something—someone—greater than your husband in your life in order to respect and love him as you should. Your incentive is the grace that has been shown you in Jesus.

Ultimately it is not about your husband's worth, his personal character, or his relative abilities as a leader. It's about the power of grace. God does not ask you to respect your husband only if he's a spiritual giant. Or when he is doing everything right. Or when he is obedient to the Word of God. Or when you believe he deserves your service. Or if he has gone a while without making any major mistakes. Or only if he is a believer. Or only if you deem him worth following. None of this is possible if it's not done in light of Christ.

Notes

1. Dr. J.R. Bruns and R.A. Richards II, "Is the Soul Mate Myth Harming Us?" *Psychology Today* (December 12, 2012), www.psychologytoday.com/repairing-relationships/201212/is-the-soul-mate-myth-harming-us.

2. John Piper, *Future Grace* (Sisters, OR: Multnomah, 1995), 336.

3. Steve Gallagher, *At the Altar of Sexual Idolatry* (Williamstown, KY: Pure Life Ministries, 2000), 31.

4. Rachel Held Evans, *A Year of Biblical Womanhood: How a Liberated Woman Found Herself Sitting on Her Roof, Covering Her Head, and Calling Her Husband "Master"* (Nashville: Thomas Nelson), 48 (Kindle ed.).

5. Held Evans, *A Year of Biblical Womanhood*, xx.

6. Held Evans, *A Year of Biblical Womanhood*, 66.

7. Held Evans, *A Year of Biblical Womanhood*, 181.

8. Bruce L. Shelley, *Church History in Plain Language* (Nashville: Thomas Nelson, 2008), 3.

9. Tim Savage, *No Ordinary Marriage* (Wheaton, IL: Crossway, 2012), 60.

10. Timothy Keller, *The Meaning of Marriage* (London: Hodder & Stoughton, 2011), 63.

11. As stated by Byron Yawn in Marcia M. Preheim, *Super(free) Woman* (CreateSpace Independent Publishing Platform, 2013), 142-3.

12. The true original source of this guide is unknown. While it's attributed to publications from the 1950s, it was probably written later. However, it does reflect to some extent perceptions and attitudes that existed in the mid-twentieth century.

13. Paul Tripp, "David: A Matter of the Heart," message given April 14, 2013, http://paultripp.com/sermons#!/swx/pp/media_archives/170495/episode/40047.

OTHER GOOD
HARVEST HOUSE READING
by Byron Forrest Yawn

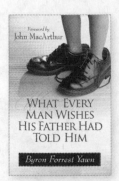

What Every Man Wishes His Father Had Told Him

What does real manhood look like?

Society can't make up its mind about what makes the ideal man. Be tougher, say some. Be more sensitive, say others. And the expectations keep changing. It doesn't help that the church plays right along.

Where can we get a clear understanding of manhood—one that's free of cultural baggage, that's actually satisfying?

Come see manhood as depicted in the Bible. Discover afresh the masculinity that pleases God, enriches marriages, and makes fatherhood the most rewarding occupation a man can know.

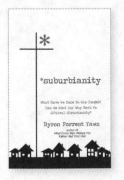

Suburbianity

What have we done to the gospel?

Within the American suburbs, countless unsuspecting and well-intended Christians miss Jesus on a weekly, if not daily, basis.

We read books. We hear sermons. We participate in Bible studies and attend conferences. But we never get around to the particulars of who Jesus is and why He did what He did. We mention Him in passing but fail to fall at His feet.

The majority of what we think is Christianity is not. Without the crucified Savior, it is not Christianity. It is Suburbianity.

Can we find our way back to true, biblical Christianity? That's what this book is about.

To learn more about Harvest House books and
to read sample chapters, log on to our website:

www.harvesthousepublishers.com

HARVEST HOUSE PUBLISHERS
EUGENE, OREGON